THE
IMMUNE
SYSTEM

GENERAL EDITORS

Dale C. Garell, M.D.

Medical Director, California Children Services, Department of Health
  Services, County of Los Angeles
Clinical Professor, Department of Pediatrics & Family Medicine,
  University of Southern California School of Medicine
Former president, Society for Adolescent Medicine

Solomon H. Snyder, M.D.

Distinguished Service Professor of Neuroscience, Pharmacology, and
  Psychiatry, Johns Hopkins University School of Medicine
Former president, Society of Neuroscience
Albert Lasker Award in Medical Research, 1978

CONSULTING EDITORS

Robert W. Blum, M.D., Ph.D.

Associate Professor, School of Public Health and Department of
  Pediatrics
Director, Adolescent Health Program, University of Minnesota
Consultant, World Health Organization

Charles E. Irwin, Jr., M.D.

Associate Professor of Pediatrics
Director, Division of Adolescent Medicine,
  University of California, San Francisco

Lloyd J. Kolbe, Ph.D.

Chief, Office of School Health & Special Projects, Center for Health
  Promotion & Education, Centers for Disease Control
President, American School Health Association

Jordan J. Popkin

Director, Division of Federal Employee Occupational Health, U.S. Public
  Health Service Region I

Joseph L. Rauh, M.D.

Professor of Pediatrics and Medicine, Adolescent Medicine, Children's
  Hospital Medical Center, Cincinnati
Former president, Society for Adolescent Medicine

THE ENCYCLOPEDIA OF
HEALTH

THE HEALTHY BODY

Dale C. Garell, M.D. · General Editor

THE
IMMUNE
SYSTEM

Edward Edelson

Introduction by C. Everett Koop, M.D., Sc.D.
Surgeon General, U.S. Public Health Service

CHELSEA HOUSE PUBLISHERS
New York · Philadelphia

The goal of the ENCYCLOPEDIA OF HEALTH *is to provide general information in the ever-changing areas of physiology, psychology, and related medical issues. The titles in this series are not intended to take the place of the professional advice of a physician or other health-care professional.*

ON THE COVER: Macrophage (a cell that fights infection) in action
Courtesy of Lennart Nilsson/Boehringer Ingelheim International

Chelsea House Publishers
EDITOR-IN-CHIEF Nancy Toff
EXECUTIVE EDITOR Remmel T. Nunn
MANAGING EDITOR Karyn Gullen Browne
COPY CHIEF Juliann Barbato
PICTURE EDITOR Adrian G. Allen
ART DIRECTOR Maria Epes
MANUFACTURING MANAGER Gerald Levine

The Encyclopedia of Health
SENIOR EDITOR Paula Edelson

Staff for THE IMMUNE SYSTEM
ASSISTANT EDITOR Laura Dolce
DEPUTY COPY CHIEF Nicole Bowen
EDITORIAL ASSISTANT Navorn Johnson
PICTURE RESEARCHER Debra P. Hershkowitz
ASSISTANT ART DIRECTOR Loraine Machlin
SENIOR DESIGNER Marjorie Zaum
PRODUCTION COORDINATOR Joseph Romano

3 5 7 9 8 6 4 2

Library of Congress Cataloging-in-Publication Data

Edelson, Edward, 1932–
THE IMMUNE SYSTEM / Edward Edelson.
  p. cm.—(The encyclopedia of health. The healthy body)
Bibliography: p.
Includes index.
ISBN 0-7910-0021-4
      0-7910-0461-9 (pbk.)
1. Immune system—Popular works. I. Title. II. Series.
QR181.7.E34 1989   89-743
616.07'9—dc 19   CIP

CONTENTS

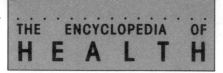

THE ENCYCLOPEDIA OF
HEALTH

THE HEALTHY BODY

The Circulatory System
Dental Health
The Digestive System
The Endocrine System
Exercise
Genetics & Heredity
The Human Body: An Overview
Hygiene
The Immune System
Memory & Learning
The Musculoskeletal System
The Neurological System
Nutrition
The Reproductive System
The Respiratory System
The Senses
Speech & Hearing
Sports Medicine
Vision
Vitamins & Minerals

THE LIFE CYCLE

Adolescence
Adulthood
Aging
Childhood
Death & Dying
The Family
Friendship & Love
Pregnancy & Birth

MEDICAL ISSUES

Careers in Health Care
Environmental Health
Folk Medicine
Health Care Delivery
Holistic Medicine
Medical Ethics
Medical Fakes & Frauds
Medical Technology
Medicine & the Law
Occupational Health
Public Health

PSYCHOLOGICAL DISORDERS AND THEIR TREATMENT

Anxiety & Phobias
Child Abuse
Compulsive Behavior
Delinquency & Criminal Behavior
Depression
Diagnosing & Treating Mental Illness
Eating Habits & Disorders
Learning Disabilities
Mental Retardation
Personality Disorders
Schizophrenia
Stress Management
Suicide

MEDICAL DISORDERS AND THEIR TREATMENT

AIDS
Allergies
Alzheimer's Disease
Arthritis
Birth Defects
Cancer
The Common Cold
Diabetes
First Aid & Emergency Medicine
Gynecological Disorders
Headaches
The Hospital
Kidney Disorders
Medical Diagnosis
The Mind-Body Connection
Mononucleosis and Other Infectious Diseases
Nuclear Medicine
Organ Transplants
Pain
Physical Handicaps
Poisons & Toxins
Prescription & OTC Drugs
Sexually Transmitted Diseases
Skin Disorders
Stroke & Heart Disease
Substance Abuse
Tropical Medicine

PREVENTION AND EDUCATION: THE KEYS TO GOOD HEALTH

C. Everett Koop, M.D., Sc.D.
Surgeon General,
U.S. Public Health Service

The issue of health education has received particular attention in recent years because of the presence of AIDS in the news. But our response to this particular tragedy points up a number of broader issues that doctors, public health officials, educators, and the public face. In particular, it points up the necessity for sound health education for citizens of all ages.

Over the past 25 years this country has been able to bring about dramatic declines in the death rates for heart disease, stroke, accidents, and, for people under the age of 45, cancer. Today, Americans generally eat better and take better care of themselves than ever before. Thus, with the help of modern science and technology, they have a better chance of surviving serious—even catastrophic—illnesses. That's the good news.

But, like every phonograph record, there's a flip side, and one with special significance for young adults. According to a report issued in 1979 by Dr. Julius Richmond, my predecessor as Surgeon General, Americans aged 15 to 24 had a higher death rate in 1979 than they did 20 years earlier. The causes: violent death and injury, alcohol and drug abuse, unwanted pregnancies, and sexually transmitted diseases. Adolescents are particularly vulnerable, because they are beginning to explore their own sexuality and perhaps to experiment with drugs. The need for educating young people is critical, and the price of neglect is high.

Yet even for the population as a whole, our health is still far from what it could be. Why? A 1974 Canadian government report attributed all death and disease to four broad elements: inadequacies in the health-care system, behavioral factors or unhealthy life-styles, environmental hazards, and human biological factors.

To be sure, there are diseases that are still beyond the control of even our advanced medical knowledge and techniques. And despite yearnings that are as old as the human race itself, there is no "fountain of youth" to ward off aging and death. Still, there is a solution to many of the problems that undermine sound health. In a word, that solution is prevention. Prevention, which includes health promotion and education, saves lives, improves the quality of life, and, in the long run, saves money.

In the United States, organized public health activities and preventive medicine have a long history. Important milestones include the improvement of sanitary procedures and the development of pasteurized milk in the late 19th century, and the introduction in the mid-20th century of effective vaccines against polio, measles, German measles, mumps, and other once-rampant diseases. Internationally, organized public health efforts began on a wide-scale basis with the International Sanitary Conference of 1851, to which 12 nations sent representatives. The World Health Organization, founded in 1948, continues these efforts under the aegis of the United Nations, with particular emphasis on combatting communicable diseases and the training of health-care workers.

But despite these accomplishments, much remains to be done in the field of prevention. For too long, we have had a medical care system that is science- and technology-based, focused, essentially, on illness and mortality. It is now patently obvious that both the social and the economic costs of such a system are becoming insupportable.

Implementing prevention—and its corollaries, health education and promotion—is the job of several groups of people:

First, the medical and scientific professions need to continue basic scientific research, and here we are making considerable progress. But increased concern with prevention will also have a decided impact on how primary-care doctors practice medicine. With a shift to health-based rather than morbidity-based medicine, the role of the "new physician" will include a healthy dose of patient education.

Second, practitioners of the social and behavioral sciences—psychologists, economists, city planners—along with lawyers, business leaders, and government officials—must solve the practical and ethical dilemmas confronting us: poverty, crime, civil rights, literacy, education, employment, housing, sanitation, environmental protection, health care delivery systems, and so forth. All of these issues affect public health.

Third is the public at large. We'll consider that very important group in a moment.

Fourth, and the linchpin in this effort, is the public health profession—doctors, epidemiologists, teachers—who must harness the professional expertise of the first two groups and the common sense and cooperation of the third, the public. They must define the problems statistically and qualitatively and then help us set priorities for finding the solutions.

To a very large extent, improving those statistics is the responsibility of every individual. So let's consider more specifically what the role of the individual should be and why health education is so important to that role. First, and most obviously, individuals can protect themselves from illness and injury and thus minimize their need for professional medical care. They can eat a nutritious diet, get adequate exercise, avoid tobacco, alcohol, and drugs, and take prudent steps to avoid accidents. The proverbial "apple a day keeps the doctor away" is not so far from the truth, after all.

Second, individuals should actively participate in their own medical care. They should schedule regular medical and dental check-ups. Should they develop an illness or injury, they should know when to treat themselves and when to seek professional help. To gain the maximum benefit from any medical treatment that they do require, individuals must become partners in that treatment. For instance, they should understand the effects and side effects of medications. I counsel young physicians that there is no such thing as too much information when talking with patients. But the corollary is the patient must know enough about the nuts and bolts of the healing process to understand what the doctor is telling him. That is at least partially the patient's responsibility.

Education is equally necessary for us to understand the ethical and public policy issues in health care today. Sometimes individuals will encounter these issues in making decisions about their own treatment or that of family members. Other citizens may encounter them as jurors in medical malpractice cases. But we all become involved, indirectly, when we elect our public officials, from school board members to the president. Should surrogate parenting be legal? To what extent is drug testing desirable, legal, or necessary? Should there be public funding for family planning, hospitals, various types of medical research, and medical care for the indigent? How should we allocate scant technological resources, such as kidney dialysis and organ transplants? What is the proper role of government in protecting the rights of patients?

What are the broad goals of public health in the United States today? In 1980, the Public Health Service issued a report aptly entitled *Promoting Health-Preventing Disease: Objectives for the Nation.* This report expressed its goals in terms of mortality and in terms of intermediate goals in education and health improvement. It identified 15 major concerns: controlling high blood pressure; improving family planning; improving pregnancy care and infant health; increasing the rate of immunization; controlling sexually transmitted diseases; controlling the presence of toxic agents and radiation in the environment; improving occupational safety and health; preventing accidents; promoting water fluoridation and dental health; controlling infectious diseases; decreasing smoking; decreasing alcohol and drug abuse; improving nutrition; promoting physical fitness and exercise; and controlling stress and violent behavior.

For healthy adolescents and young adults (ages 15 to 24), the specific goal was a 20% reduction in deaths, with a special focus on motor vehicle injuries and alcohol and drug abuse. For adults (ages 25 to 64), the aim was 25% fewer deaths, with a concentration on heart attacks, strokes, and cancers.

Smoking is perhaps the best example of how individual behavior can have a direct impact on health. Today cigarette smoking is recognized as the most important single preventable cause of death in our society. It is responsible for more cancers and more cancer deaths than any other known agent; is a prime risk factor for heart and blood vessel disease, chronic bronchitis, and emphysema; and is a frequent cause of complications in pregnancies and of babies born prematurely, underweight, or with potentially fatal respiratory and cardiovascular problems.

Since the release of the Surgeon General's first report on smoking in 1964, the proportion of adult smokers has declined substantially, from 43% in 1965 to 30.5% in 1985. Since 1965, 37 million people have quit smoking. Although there is still much work to be done if we are to become a "smoke-free society," it is heartening to note that public health and public education efforts—such as warnings on cigarette packages and bans on broadcast advertising—have already had significant effects.

In 1835, Alexis de Tocqueville, a French visitor to America, wrote, "In America the passion for physical well-being is general." Today, as then, health and fitness are front-page items. But with the greater scientific and technological resources now available to us, we are in a far stronger position to make good health care available to everyone. And with the greater technological threats to us as we approach the 21st century, the need to do so is more urgent than ever before. Comprehensive information about basic biology, preventive medicine, medical and surgical treatments, and related ethical and public policy issues can help you arm yourself with the knowledge you need to be healthy throughout your life.

FOREWORD

Dale C. Garell, M.D.

Advances in our understanding of health and disease during the 20th century have been truly remarkable. Indeed, it could be argued that modern health care is one of the greatest accomplishments in all of human history. In the early 1900s, improvements in sanitation, water treatment, and sewage disposal reduced death rates and increased longevity. Previously untreatable illnesses can now be managed with antibiotics, immunizations, and modern surgical techniques. Discoveries in the fields of immunology, genetic diagnosis, and organ transplantation are revolutionizing the prevention and treatment of disease. Modern medicine is even making inroads against cancer and heart disease, two of the leading causes of death in the United States.

Although there is much to be proud of, medicine continues to face enormous challenges. Science has vanquished diseases such as smallpox and polio, but new killers, most notably AIDS, confront us. Morcover, we now victimize ourselves with what some have called "diseases of choice," or those brought on by drug and alcohol abusc, bad eating habits, and mismanagement of the stresses and strains of contemporary life. The very technology that is doing so much to prolong life has brought with it previously unimaginable ethical dilemmas related to issues of death and dying. The rising cost of health-care is a matter of central concern to us all. And violence in the form of automobile accidents, homicide, and suicide remain the major killers of young adults.

In thc past, most people were content to leave health care and medical treatment in the hands of professionals. But since the 1960s, the consumer of medical care—that is, the patient—has assumed an increasingly central role in the management of his or her own health. There has also been a new emphasis placed on prevention: People are recognizing that their own actions can help prevent many of the conditions that have caused death and disease in the past. This accounts for the growing commitment to good nutrition and regular exercise, for the fact that more and more people are choosing not to smoke, and for a new moderation in people's drinking habits.

11

People want to know more about themselves and their own health. They are curious about their body: its anatomy, physiology, and biochemistry. They want to keep up with rapidly evolving medical technologies and procedures. They are willing to educate themselves about common disorders and diseases so that they can be full partners in their own health-care.

The ENCYCLOPEDIA OF HEALTH is designed to provide the basic knowledge that readers will need if they are to take significant responsibility for their own health. It is also meant to serve as a frame of reference for further study and exploration. The ENCYCLOPEDIA is divided into five subsections: The Healthy Body; The Life Cycle; Medical Disorders & Their Treatment; Psychological Disorders & Their Treatment; and Medical Issues. For each topic covered by the ENCYCLOPEDIA, we present the essential facts about the relevant biology; the symptoms, diagnosis, and treatment of common diseases and disorders; and ways in which you can prevent or reduce the severity of health problems when that is possible. The ENCYCLOPEDIA also projects what may lie ahead in the way of future treatment or prevention strategies.

The broad range of topics and issues covered in the ENCYCLOPEDIA reflects the fact that human health encompasses physical, psychological, social, environmental, and spiritual well-being. Just as the mind and the body are inextricably linked, so, too, is the individual an integral part of the wider world that comprises his or her family, society, and environment. To discuss health in its broadest aspect it is necessary to explore the many ways in which it is connected to such fields as law, social science, public policy, economics, and even religion. And so, the ENCYCLOPEDIA is meant to be a bridge between science, medical technology, the world at large, and you. I hope that it will inspire you to pursue in greater depth particular areas of interest, and that you will take advantage of the suggestions for further reading and the lists of resources and organizations that can provide additional information.

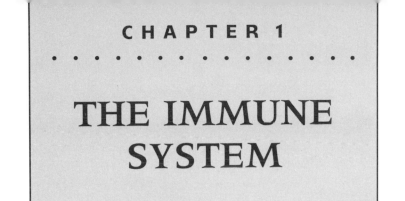

CHAPTER 1

. . . .

THE IMMUNE SYSTEM

David "the boy in a bubble."

The immune system is a collection of tissues, cells, and molecules working together to recognize and attack the small enemies that prowl about the world, looking for ways to make biological profit at the expense of the human body.

A good way to appreciate what the immune system does is to think about the common cold. This annoying ailment causes the sufferer to sneeze, sniffle, and ache. The misery is tolerable because the victim knows it will go away in a week or so. Some people, however, do not get better. In fact, the slightest infection can prove deadly to them. The reason is that they lack a functioning immune system, which means their bodies cannot rally to fight off the viruses that cause the common cold. These people can be kept alive only by drastic measures, such as being kept in an absolutely germfree environment. One such child was a boy named David, who became known as "the boy in a bubble." Born in 1971 with no immune defenses, he was delivered in a germfree environment at a hospital in Houston. His life was prolonged, but at a heavy cost: He had to be isolated 24 hours a day in a small, absolutely sterile environment. David died in his early teens when a bone marrow transplant failed.

THE DEFENSES OF THE IMMUNE SYSTEM

Most people usually need only a week for their immune system to expel the enemy responsible for the discomfort that accompanies a cold. During this week, the immune system builds cel-

A microphotograph of cells infected with a common cold virus. Viruses cannot be seen with the naked eye. The round and near-round structures seen in the photograph are not found in uninfected cells.

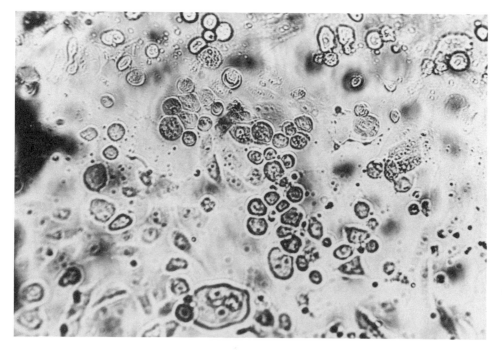

lular and molecular defenses that eventually overcome the virus and rid the body of its infection. Moreover, the system stores the knowledge that one specific virus caused the infection; should it invade again, the virus will be overwhelmed before it can cause more mischief. (The reason people suffer from so many colds is that a different virus causes each one.)

Knowledge of the Immune System

The preceding paragraph could have been written half a century ago. At that time, scientists had a broad knowledge of the way the immune system works. They knew the body has two lines of defense, one made of cells and the other of molecules called antibodies. Indeed, knowledge of cellular immunity goes back as far as 1883, when a Russian biologist, Élie Metchnikoff, discovered phagocytes, a type of white blood cell that attacks and engulfs bacteria. Knowledge about molecular defenses dates back nearly as far. In the late 19th century—soon after the first vaccines were developed from tissue that contained the agents of disease—the German bacteriologist Paul Ehrlich recognized that these vaccines worked because they stimulated an antibody response. By the 1920s, biologists knew that antibodies were a form of protein.

It was not until the early 1960s, however, that researchers puzzled out the mechanism by which the body can produce an almost infinite variety of antibodies, one for each invader. And much of what this book describes depends on knowledge acquired in the 1970s and 1980s. Progress toward a full understanding of the immune system has occurred at a steadily quickening rate as more scientists explore the subject and as their techniques become more advanced. It is now known that the immune system consists of a highly complex interlinking of cellular and molecular activities, in which cells produce molecules that stimulate other cells to produce other molecules that stimulate still other cells to multiply. And there is more to learn, as new interactions are discovered and analyzed.

Immunologists already know a great deal, however. They can start with a stem cell (a single primitive immune cell produced in the bone marrow), follow it as it multiplies, track the offspring that migrate to different parts of the body, and by observing the

In the late 19th century, German bacteriologist Paul Ehrlich discovered that vaccines work by stimulating an antibody response in the body.

many different functions these offspring perform, identify particular offspring. Scientists can also identify and classify the molecular components of the system, which include not only antibodies but also major new classes of molecules—cytokines and lymphokines and interleukins.

Some fruits of this basic research are already being put to practical use described in later chapters of this book. A type of interleukin is being used to treat some forms of cancer. Interferon, which is one of the cytokines, is also employed in some cancer treatments. Laboratory-manufactured molecules called monoclonal antibodies are being used in a rapidly growing number of diagnostic tests; they also have other medical uses.

It is important to remember, however, that basic research findings do not move directly from the laboratory to general medical use. In fact, most of the practical medical uses of immunological knowledge—polio vaccines, allergy treatments, and more—derive from findings that are decades old.

There is no better example of this time lag than that presented by acquired immune deficiency syndrome (AIDS). AIDS was identified in April 1981 through some intelligent medical detective work. Since then, researchers have learned that it is a disease of the immune system; have identified the virus that causes it; have shown exactly how that virus spreads; and have developed a number of strategies for fighting the virus. But as of 1989, only one drug, azidothymidine (AZT), has shown some effectiveness against the AIDS virus, and that was a failed cancer drug that a researcher simply took down from the shelf. Efforts to develop a vaccine against AIDS have been slow and tortuous.

Even so, immunologists today have a better understanding of the workings of the immune system than ever before, and thus they have a better chance of manipulating it to improve its workings and correct any flaws. Consider, again, the story of the viruses that cause the common cold.

Viruses

In immunological terms, a virus consists of a core of genetic material, either RNA or DNA, wrapped in a coat made of proteins. Among these proteins are molecules called antigens. When a cold-causing virus enters the body, the immune system recognizes the presence of antigens that are different from those already existing in the body and homes in on them.

Upon entering the bloodstream, the virus encounters a macrophage, one of the many different kinds of immune system cells. The macrophage absorbs the virus and displays the viral antigens on the outer surface of its cell membrane. That display attracts two other kinds of immune system cells, B cells and T cells, each of which has a specific function.

Two Types of Cells

B cells are partly responsible for what immunologists call humoral immunity; that is, they produce antibodies. Once a foreign antigen is recognized by a B cell, the cell multiplies and changes into an antibody-producing factory. It becomes a plasma cell and turns out large quantities of antibodies that combat a specific antigen of the cold virus. These antibody molecules combine with the virus and inactivate it.

T cells are responsible for cellular immunity. They play a role in this process—several roles, in fact, because there are several types of T cells. One kind, called a helper T cell, helps activate the immune system by giving off signals that set antibody-producing B cells and other components of the immune system into action. Another type of T cell, a suppressor T cell, modulates the immune response so the body will not be overwhelmed. Other T cells secrete lymphokines, molecules that, among other functions, attract more immune cells to the site of the infection and help control their activity when they get there.

Yet another subset of T cells is the killer T cell. Its role is to destroy the carrier of the alien antigen. Killer T cells aim to destroy any foreign element, including transplanted organs, such as kidneys and hearts. For this reason transplants did not become successful until doctors learned how to stop killer T cells without damaging the other parts of the immune response.

By the time the cold sufferer is feeling completely miserable, the cold virus is under attack by both the cellular and humoral parts of the immune system. In less than a week, the viral invader is overcome. The antibody-producing plasma cells stop their efforts, but the immune system retains a memory of the invasion, in the form of sensitized B cells. Should the same cold virus invade the body again, it will be overwhelmed before it can do great damage.

IMMUNE RESPONSES

This simplified scenario helps explain many aspects of the immune response: how it protects people, how it can go wrong, and—perhaps most important—how scientists manipulate it to prevent and cure illness. The most common kind of manipulation is immunization, in which a killed or weakened form of an infectious agent is administered into the body, usually by injection. This vaccine does not cause a person to get sick, but it puts the immune system on alert, so that it will be ready to pounce should the actual agent of infection enter the body.

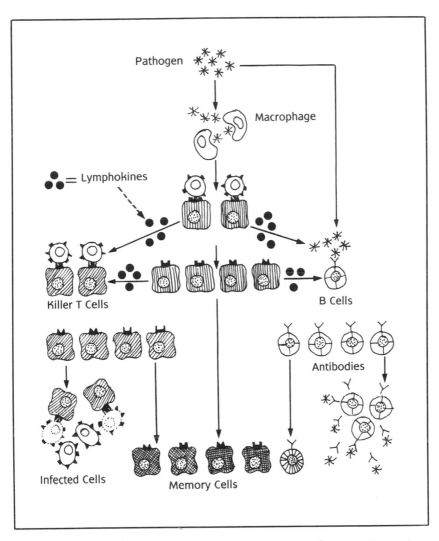

Macrophages engulf immune system intruders, or pathogens, then relay their antigenic components (internal components are represented as square; external as triangular) to receptors on T cells. Helper T4 cells then multiply and release lymphokines, which regulate both B and T cells. Interaction with T cells and macrophages motivates the killer T8 cells to mature and roam the bloodstream, destroying the infected cells. At the same time, external antigens on the pathogen interact with B-cell receptors. If the B cells receive signals from the lymphokines, they reproduce antibodies that bind to the antigens, neutralizing them. Memory cells (antigen-specific) are also created, ensuring that the immune sytem will more effectively deal with the same pathogen in the future.

Allergies and Autoimmune Responses

The activities that occur inside the body when someone catches a cold also occur when someone has an allergy. The difference is that in the case of an allergy, the immune system reacts—for unknown reasons—to something harmless, such as an antigen carried on ragweed pollen or animal hair. A similarly misguided response occurs in the case of autoimmune diseases, in which the immune system somehow regards the body's own tissue as foreign and attacks it. Autoimmune diseases include rheumatoid arthritis, multiple sclerosis, and myasthenia gravis. One form of diabetes, type I diabetes mellitus, also seems to be caused by an autoimmune response.

There are also immune disorders caused by over- or under-activity of specific components of the immune system. AIDS is one such disease. It occurs when the human immunodeficiency virus (HIV) kills helper T cells, knocking out most immune system activity and leaving the body vulnerable to a number of otherwise harmless microbes as well as to some kinds of cancer and other diseases.

The Role of Genetics

Autoimmune diseases tell us that genetics—our inherited traits—figures crucially in immunology. The genes people inherit from their parents place markers, called HLA or MHC antigens, on all body tissues, identifying them as parts of the body that the immune system should not attack. Essential as these markers are, they can cause difficulties, especially for people who need new organs. If a new heart or liver is installed, the body may react violently to it. Thus, before surgeons can install the new organ, they must find a donor whose tissue matches up well with the patient's. The closest match is between identical twins, because their genetic makeup is identical. Brothers and sisters come next, followed by parents and other close relatives. But because of the way nature tosses the genetic dice, it is possible for total strangers to have closely matched HLA antigens. Blood tests can tell how close the match is.

Genetics also affects the immune system's response to anything from ragweed pollen to viruses to environmental pollutants. Scientists have begun to puzzle out the molecular operation of these responses. They have gleaned some insight, for instance, into how certain allergic reactions occur, thus enabling doctors to prevent or reduce them. But for the most part, allergies remain a mystery. No one knows, for instance, why the immune system in some 40 million Americans singles out ragweed pollen or other allergens for attack. And researchers are just beginning to get an inkling of the interactions that cause autoimmune diseases.

Genetic peculiarities that govern the immunological reaction to viruses seem to be involved in some autoimmune diseases. One example is subacute sclerosing panencephalitis, a disease that can be triggered by the measles vaccine. Most people do not react strongly to the measles virus vaccine. But about one person in a million suffers badly from it: Somehow the virus contained in the vaccine burrows into nerve cells and sets off an autoimmune response that causes the body to deteriorate and die. It is now believed that rheumatoid arthritis, diabetes, and other autoimmune diseases are also caused by reactions to certain viruses. The case is far from proved, however.

Tissue typing, shown here, measures the similarity in the genetic material of different people. This process helps ensure a healthy transplant operation and minimizes the threat of rejection.

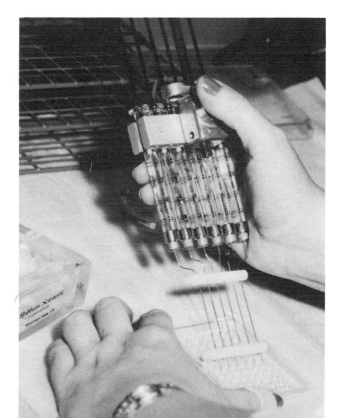

A BRAND-NEW FIELD

There may be an altogether different reason why some people's immune systems malfunction. This possibility has given rise to a brand-new, controversial field of research known by one of two jawbreaking names—*psychoneuroimmunology* or *neuroimmunomodulation*. Researchers in this field study how emotions affect the immune system. Their findings are controversial and will probably be much revised, but so far experts in the field have shown that a person's feelings can influence the way in which his or her body produces hormones, which in turn influences the strength of the immune response. Some studies show that people who are under stress—because they have lost a job or a loved one or for some other reason—are especially prone to illness. For example, a study at Columbia University found lowered immune system activity in men whose wives had recently died, and a study of medical students at Ohio State University found that concentrations of a key immune system cell decreased just before examinations, a stressful time for the students. Debate surrounds these studies, but research continues.

Before probing the latest in scientific research, this book will examine the basics of immunology, starting with the cells of the immune system.

•   •   •   •

CHAPTER 2

THE CELLS

B lymphocytes as seen through an electron microscope.

The human immune system is a complicated one; it developed gradually from simpler systems, keeping many of them intact and adding features over many millions of years. For this reason, scientists have increased their knowledge of the human immune system by examining other organisms, even those as simple as sponges and worms, whose ancestors existed millions of years before the first mammals made their appearance on earth. These

23

primitive beings faced the attacks of potentially hostile microbes and developed defenses so successful that as humans developed, they retained these mechanisms, although the human body also includes other defenses that do not exist in simpler animals.

PIECE BY PIECE

The immune system can be understood more easily if it is approached piece by piece, though it is important to remember that these pieces, like the system itself, do not work in isolation. The best place to start is with the cells. They coordinate with immune molecules: Cells sometimes produce molecular activity and molecules sometimes produce cellular activity.

The B cells and T cells, discussed in Chapter 1, arrived fairly recently in the evolution of immune systems. The human body also contains more primitive types of immune cells whose relatives are found in invertebrates, which have existed for billions of years. B cells and T cells have relatively sophisticated ways of attacking invaders, whereas more primitive cells just eat them.

In mammals, primitive immune cells, like B and T cells, originate in the bone marrow, the soft, pulpy matter located in the hollow center of the body's long bones. The process of creating these cells begins with the most basic kind of cell, the stem cell. There are relatively few stem cells in the bone marrow, perhaps one out of every two or three thousand. Thus, it was a major achievement when in 1988 Irving Weisman of Stanford University isolated stem cells for the first time—in a mouse. This breakthrough was a very important step forward in understanding the immune system.

Macrophages

One type of primitive cell, the macrophage, develops from cells called monocytes, which develop from stem cells and are situated in the blood. Macrophages not only eat invaders but also process them so they can be attacked by B cells and T cells. Macrophages act in a variety of ways. Some drift continually through the body, on the lookout for unwelcome agents. Others attach themselves

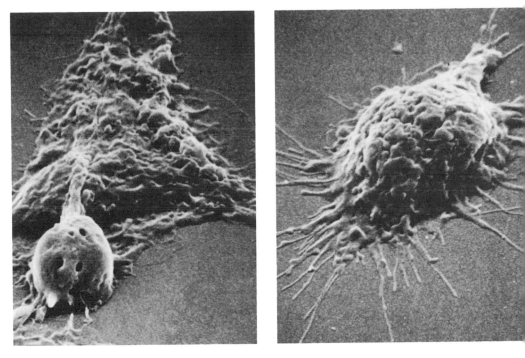

A macrophage (far left) moves in on and engulfs a cancer cell. Macrophages not only eat invaders, but also process them so that they can be attacked by B and T cells.

to specific tissues, such as the liver and spleen, and lie in wait there, like a border patrol prepared for an attack. These stationary macrophages help compose the reticuloendothelial system.

Phagocytes

All macrophages are phagocytes (*phagocyte* derives from the Greek word for eating). Other, more common phagocytes, such as granulocytes, seem to function within the immune system as a first line of defense. They head directly toward infected areas and engulf invading microbes, which they kill by digesting them, using killer enzymes carried in small units called lysosomes. These enzymes are also carried by immune cells that attack invaders that are too big to be eaten. The cells emit granules containing the defensive enzymes, which then attack the invader directly or indirectly. For example, a cell called the eosinophil has an enzyme that can break down the body walls of parasites. Related cells, basophils and mast cells, release chemical messengers that either attract other immune system cells to the site or produce a local reaction that makes blood vessels leaky.

The chemicals that cause these reactions, called mediators, include histamine and other chemicals called leukotrienes and prostaglandins. Mediator release is responsible for the reactions that help the body fight infectious agents but also cause reddening and swelling. Mediators can also be released when the immune system mistakes an innocuous invader for a dangerous one. That mistake is an allergic reaction.

Another feature of the primitive immune system is a family of proteins called complement proteins. They have a number of varied functions. One is to attract phagocytes to an invader and then make them become more active. This is one of many examples of how immune cells (the phagocytes) and molecules (the proteins) work together.

A Family of Cells

Just as a stem cell reproduces, so it specializes, spawning descendants that follow one of two paths. One path leads them to become macrophages, mast cells, eosinophils, and other primitive cells. The other path leads them to become lymphocytes, of which there are three general types: B cells, T cells, and null cells.

The best-known null cells are natural killer cells, whose function is simple, direct, and easy to describe. When they encounter something unfamiliar, they attack it immediately, without any prompting, although they move more ferociously if stimulated by chemical signals from other immune cells.

B cells and T cells require more explanation. The best way to begin is by describing how stem cells become B cells and T cells. A stem cell is more likely to follow this path of development if, during its growth, it migrates to certain areas of the body. Some stem cells migrate to the thymus, a small organ in the upper part of the chest, behind the breastbone. They become T cells (the *T* comes from *thymus*). Stem cells become B cells if they mature either in the bone marrow or in organs of the lymph system.

THE LYMPH SYSTEM

The lymph system is the collection of organs that help make up the immune system. It includes the bone marrow, the thymus, the spleen, the tonsils, and the lymph nodes. These last are small structures found throughout the body and linked by a network of lymphatic vessels, through which flows a honey-colored fluid called lymph. Any virus or bacterium that enters the body reaches the lymph and eventually passes through a lymph node, which can become inflamed, causing the "swollen glands" you feel in your neck when you have a cold or other infection. When lymph nodes are inflamed, it means that B cells and T cells are reacting to an invader. Lymph nodes are meeting places for antigens and lymphocytes. Circulating B cells and T cells are squeezed tightly together as they pass through a lymph node. If a foreign antigen also happens to be there, the body reacts quickly.

Self-antigens

The way to understand how B cells work is to start with T cells. As previously mentioned, T cells originate as stem cells that migrate to the thymus. There they mature and acquire the remarkable ability to distinguish between the body's own antigens and foreign ones. The body has two kinds of self-antigens: type 1 antigens are carried on all cells of the body; type 2 antigens are carried only on macrophages and a few other immune cells.

It is not yet known what exactly happens to T cells as they mature in the thymus. It appears, however, that a selection process occurs in which immature T cells that attack the body's own tissue (type 1 antigens) are destroyed. What remain are T cells that are not bred to attack the type 1 antigens they may encounter. This process of elimination does not always work perfectly. In certain people with defective immune systems, some T cells can react against the body's own tissues. This is an important feature of autoimmune diseases, the subject of a later chapter in this book.

Three Populations

There are three major populations of T cells: killer (formally, cytotoxic) T cells, which attack and destroy strange cells directly;

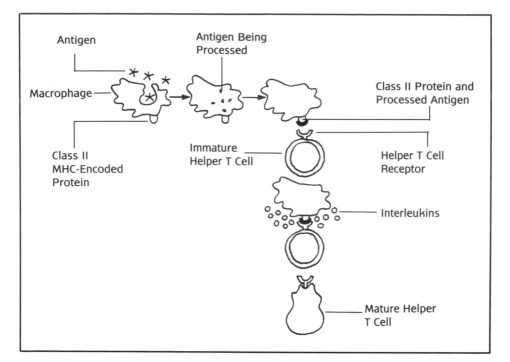

Killer T cells are activated by a different process from that of helper T cells. Although antigen fragments are present, they combine with class I proteins; the killer T cell then matures with the assistance of a helper T cell.

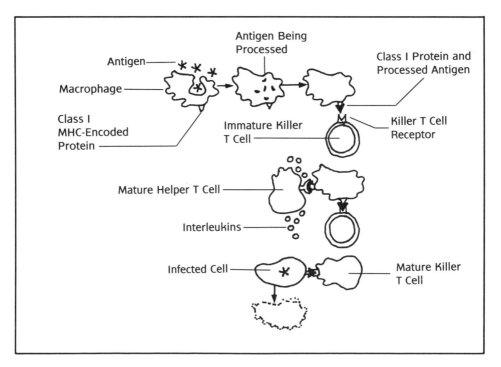

helper T cells, which stimulate a defensive response by B cells and other T cells; and suppressor T cells, which turn off the defensive response at the appropriate time.

T cells remain inactive until they have received the special signals already described. This sets them apart from other weapons in the immune system arsenal, which go to work the instant they encounter a foreign antigen. A phagocyte or a null cell begins its attack immediately upon recognizing an antigen located, as most are, on the exterior of the invading organism—on the coat of a virus, for example, or on the membrane of a bacterium. A T cell will not attack, however, until the offending antigen has been processed in a way that alerts the entire genetic apparatus of the immune response.

The discussion of the common cold in Chapter 1 mentioned that the immune system goes into action when a macrophage engulfs a cold virus and displays the virus's antigens on its cell surface. That step requires that the foreign antigen be presented in combination with a self-antigen, either one of the major histocompatibility complex (MHC) antigens or one of the human leukocyte antigens (HLA). These antigens are produced by a set of immune system genes, also called MHC or HLA genes.

MHC and HLA Genes

Major histocompatibility complex antigens got their name because they were originally discovered (by various scientists in the 1930s) to be the antigens that trigger attacks made against foreign cells. Since then, scientists have learned that the MHC antigens play an essential role in all the immune responses of T cells, which will not respond to a foreign antigen unless it appears in combination with a MHC protein on the surface of a cell.

Two requirements must be met before T cells attack. The first is that a T cell must recognize the body's own type 1 MHC proteins. The second is that the foreign antigens must be accompanied by type 2 antigens. This system of checks lessens the chance the immune system will mistakenly attack the cells of its own tissues.

Killer T cells are triggered by the combination of a type 1 MHC antigen and a foreign antigen. They attack the instant they recognize viral antigens displayed on the surface of an infected cell alongside its type 1 antigens.

Helper T cells are triggered by the combination of a type 2 MHC antigen and a foreign antigen. They then send out signals that bring the rest of the immune system into action.

T cells have receptors on their membrane that respond when they sense the presence of an appropriate combination of foreign antigen and self-antigen. Each T cell is so individual that it can be activated by only one antigen. This may seem wasteful, because there are so many antigens, but it makes sense because there are also many lymphocytes in the body.

Into Action

Once a T cell meets its antigen, it goes into action. Activated T cells multiply into a number large enough to fight the invader. Exactly what action a T cell takes depends on the type of cell it is. A killer T cell attacks any cell displaying the cytotoxic antigen. A helper T cell sends out chemical signals in the form of lymphokines, molecules that alert other cells of the immune system, notably B cells. Suppressor T cells do not match up with a specific foe but rather regulate the immune response, so that the body is not damaged by an overzealous attack of its own forces.

The lymphokines—which will be discussed in greater detail in Chapter 4—also affect how B cells operate. Indeed, lymphokines are essential to B-cell activity. B cells have some receptors that allow them to recognize a few antigens, but they mostly depend on signals from T cells to begin their all-important activity: producing antibodies.

An antibody is a protein manufactured to fight one specific antigen. It combines with that antigen, and no other, and puts it out of commission. Since the 1920s, scientists have known that one antibody exists to meet every antigen, but not until the 1950s could scientists explain why. What defied explanation was how the B cells could possibly be ready to produce antibodies for what is an overwhelming number of antigens.

How B Cells Work

One theory held that the body contained a store of all the antibodies it would ever need and that the appearance of an antigen
increased production of the specific antibody needed to combat
it. This theory was flawed, however, because it required the body
to contain an almost infinite number of antibodies. The alternate
theory, proved true in the 1950s, holds that the body has antibody-producing cells that can alter their manner of production
and thus create whatever antibody it needs. (The structure and
operation of antibodies are discussed in Chapter 3.)

In a B cell, the production line for antibodies starts in the cell
nucleus, where the genes are located. A gene is a section of a
long molecule, either deoxyribonucleic acid (DNA) or ribonucleic

*B cells transpose their genes to battle specific antigens. Once this pro-
cess takes place, the B cells become plasma cells, which then produce
antibodies.*

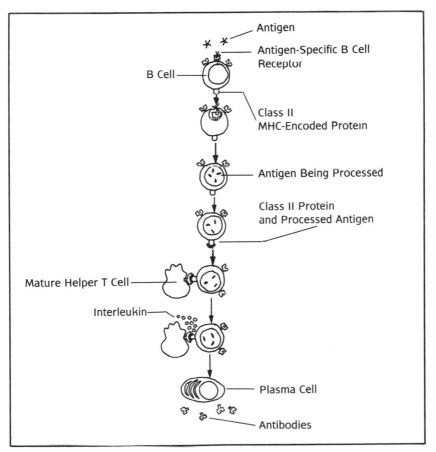

acid (RNA), in which the sequence of nitrogenous bases determines the structure of a protein made by the cell. Given that any cell contains a finite number of genes, how can it manufacture an almost infinite variety of antibodies?

The answer is that the antibody genes of a B cell can change in response to the challenge posed by a specific antigen. When a B cell responds to a lymphokine from an activated T cell, it shuffles its antibody genes so they produce exactly the antibody needed to fight the antigen. Some subunits of the gene are dropped, others combine to form a unique sequence that codes for a unique protein. This ability to shuffle genes is the key to antibody production, the reason why B cells can extract an almost infinite variety of antibodies from a finite source of genetic material. An identical shuffling of genes occurs in T cells and allows the T cell to produce all the receptors needed to respond to antigens.

Once the genes are shuffled, the activated B cell changes into what is called a plasma cell. This means it becomes an antibody factory, multiplying itself and secreting large amounts of the antibody until signals from suppressor T cells indicate that the invasion has been repulsed. The number of plasma cells producing the antibody drops sharply, but B cells whose receptors deal with the specific antigen remain in the blood, ready for action should the antigen appear again. A few T cells with the same kind of receptor also remain and meet the same purpose. This immune memory is the reason why vaccines prevent disease.

This briefly describes how antibodies are made. The next chapter explains what they are and how they work.

•   •   •   •

CHAPTER 3

MOLECULES I: ANTIBODIES

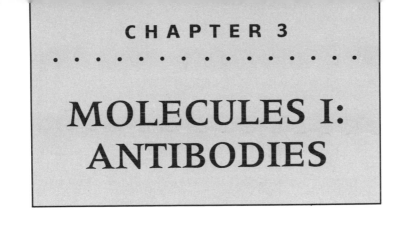

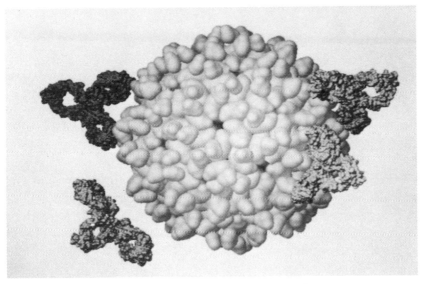

A computer graphic of a hypothetical antibody attack.

One of the most outstanding scientific achievements of the 1980s has been the ability to manufacture made-to-order antibodies. It has become routine work for laboratories to churn out large quantities of the specific antibody needed to combat almost any given antigen. These monoclonal antibodies have already had a revolutionary impact on biology and medicine. They are being used to diagnose disease, treat cancer, fight AIDS, and to help biologists in their basic research.

The scientists Cesar Milstein and George Kohler, who invented the method for making monoclonal antibodies, received many awards for their feat, including the most prestigious of all, the Nobel Prize. But these researchers stand on the shoulders of many biologists who paved the way with their research on antibodies. It would be impossible to make a monoclonal antibody without knowing what an antibody is, how the body makes it, how it functions, and so on.

WHAT IS AN ANTIBODY?

An antibody is a protein, a large molecule made up of smaller units called amino acids. A protein can be likened to a chain in which the amino acids form the various links. A basic antibody molecule actually consists of four chains of amino acids, in two sets. There are two heavy (H) chains and two light (L) chains. The molecule has two identical long chains and two identical short chains, joined together in a Y shape. Both the long chains and the short chains in all antibodies have segments (called constant regions) that are identical in composition to that segment in other antibodies of a given class. They also have variable regions, in which the composition differs in antibodies made to attack different antigens.

The variable regions include small sections, called hypervariable regions, that enable an antibody to single out one antigen for attack. Hypervariable regions are located in the part of the antibody called the antigen binding site, which clamps the antibody to the antigen. The antigen binding site is located in the fork-shaped part of the Y.

Antibody-antigen binding works like a lock and key. An antibody recognizes an antigen by its shape, and the hypervariable regions allow the antibody to mold itself to fit that shape. The antibody can then combine with the antigen, a crucial step in the immune response. The antibody inactivates the antigen directly, antibody-antigen complexes form, and the process sets off other defensive mechanisms. (One such mechanism, the complement system, is discussed in Chapter 4.)

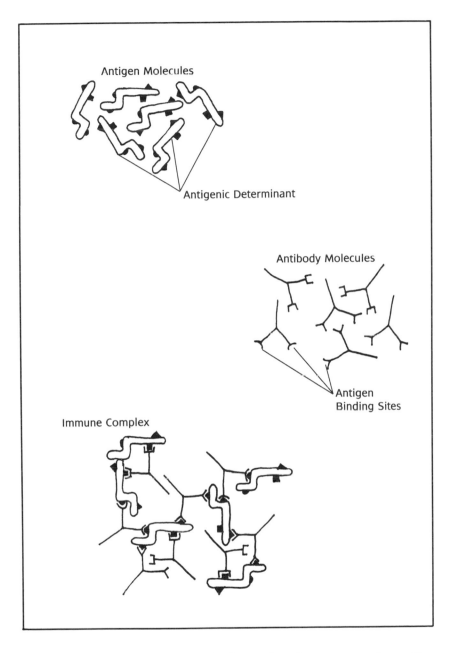

Antigen molecules bind with antibodies to form immune complexes. The antigenic determinants fit into antigen binding sites much like a key opening a locked door.

Immunoglobulin

Collectively, antibodies belong to a group of proteins called immunoglobulin, so named because they belong to the immune system and have a globular shape. Within this group, researchers have discovered five classes of antibodies. Each has a slightly different kind of chain, each functions differently in the body, and some differ in the number of Y-shaped units they have. The five classes include the following:

1. *Immunoglobulin G* (abbreviated IgG): Accounting for about 75% of all the immunoglobulin in the blood, it consists of a single Y-shaped unit. It is the substance administered when someone gets a shot of gamma globulin to fight or prevent an infection.

Students line up in 1953 for gamma globulin vaccines. Gamma globulin is another term for immunoglobulin G, an antibody that accounts for almost 75% of all immunoglobulins in the blood.

2. *Immunoglobulin M* (IgM): It consists of five Y-shaped units that radiate out from a common center.

3. *Immunoglobulin A* (IgA): It exists in three different forms, which have one, two, or three Y-shaped units. Large quantities of the two-unit form appear in saliva and tears.

4. *Immunoglobulin D* (IgD): It has one Y-shaped unit. Although it is not commonly found in blood, it does appear on the membrane of B cells and is believed to play a role in their response to antigens.

5. *Immunoglobulin E* (IgE): It has one Y-shaped unit and is immensely important because it is responsible for allergic reactions.

ANTIBODIES

Why are there so many kinds of antibodies? One reason is that they tend to congregate in different locations: IgA is found in tears and saliva, IgD shows up mostly on the surface of B cells, and so on. A second reason is that each antibody has a special function. The body responds to one kind of infection primarily by producing IgM, to another kind by producing mostly IgG. The function of IgE is to attack large parasites. It attaches itself to them and to mast cells and basophils simultaneously.

This cross-linking causes the release of mediators such as histamine that produce the condition known as inflammation. Inflammation is painful, but it is an effective way for the body to kill harmful invaders. However, a problem arises when this protective mechanism is set off by invaders, such as ragweed pollen, that pose no threat. That mistaken response is called allergy, and is discussed at greater length in Chapter 6.

There is yet another major reason why there are so many kinds of antibodies. The wide variety allows antibodies to recognize and attack epitopes, which are the different sections of an antigen. For instance, IgM attacks one epitope of viral antigen while IgG attacks another, thus ensuring that the invader does not slip through the defense system.

Clonal Selection

The process by which a B cell is alerted to an antigen, divides rapidly, and converts to antibody-producing plasma cells is called clonal selection. A clone is a large number of cells that are identical because they originate from a single cell. In popular usage, *clone* has come to refer to a human manufactured in a laboratory to resemble another person. In fact, *clone* is a matter-of-fact term used every day by scientists who work closely with cells. Cloning happens whenever someone's B cells respond to an infection.

The mass production of a single antibody directed against a specific antigen is called monoclonal antibody technology. *Monoclonal* means that the antibodies are produced by a single clone of cells made to order in the laboratory. Hundreds of laboratories now work on them and they are revolutionizing medical practice and scientific research.

A Daring Idea

The monoclonal antibody story began in the early 1970s, when Cesar Milstein, a geneticist at Cambridge University in England, was studying the genetics of antibody production. He wanted to learn the number of genes involved in that process because he had been given a line of mouse cancer cells that produced a single antibody. He asked one of his assistants, George Kohler, to find the antigen for that antibody.

Kohler got nowhere, but he had a daring idea. Instead of starting with an antibody, why not start with an antigen and produce a clone of cells that made an antibody to it? Accordingly, Kohler injected an antigen into a mouse, extracted the antibody-producing B cells from the mouse, fused them with cancer cells, and then isolated a clone of cells capable of making the antibody that fought the injected antigen.

The really innovative part of the scheme was the idea of combining an ordinary B cell with a cancer cell. Lines of B cells, like all other normal cell lines, are mortal. For a time, the cells reproduce, but sooner or later the cell line loses this capability and dies. Lines of cancer cells, however, do not die naturally. These cells are dangerous not because they reproduce so fast but be-

Dr. Cesar Milstein, one of the discoverers of the monoclonal antibody, which aids scientists in diagnosing some conditions and can help prevent transplant patients from rejecting their new organs.

cause they never stop reproducing. Somehow, they have lost the natural controls that make a cell stop dividing. The fusion of a normal B cell and a cancer cell—called hybridoma—leads to a cell line that produces an antibody forever.

Kohler made the hybridoma by using the mouse's B cells formed in response to the antigen injection (in this case, sheep red blood cells) and cells from a mouse myeloma, a bone cancer. In 1975, he and Milstein reported their success in a scientific paper. "Such cells," they announced, "can be grown in massive cultures to provide specific antibody. Such cultures could be valuable for medical and industrial use."

These words had a tremendous impact. In 1981, a scientific panel asked by the U.S. Food and Drug Administration (FDA) to evaluate new medical technologies described monoclonal antibodies as probably "the most useful biomedical discovery for the rest of the century." By 1989, monoclonal antibodies had become the basis of a billion-dollar industry that was growing rapidly.

Using Monoclonal Antibodies

The primary use of monoclonal antibodies is in diagnostic tests. For example, home pregnancy tests use a monoclonal antibody to detect a protein hormone produced by women only when they are pregnant. Other tests, conducted in doctors' offices and hospitals, detect the antigens whose presence leads to a diagnosis of hepatitis, heart attack, infection, and other illnesses. The hepatitis test looks for an antigen on the hepatitis virus; the heart attack test looks for a protein that is produced by damaged heart-muscle cells, and so on.

Diagnostic use of monoclonal antibodies has proceeded at a faster rate than has treatment use. The first monoclonal antibody used routinely in therapy was OKT3, a product that can help prevent patients from rejecting transplanted organs. OKT3 is an antibody that binds with certain receptors of T cells—called T3 receptors—and thus prevents them from attacking the cells of the transplanted kidney, liver, heart, or other organ.

Developing Treatments

Researchers have employed a similar strategy to develop a treatment for multiple sclerosis and other autoimmune diseases. Recent evidence has shown that multiple sclerosis occurs when a subset of T cells attacks the body's own tissue—specifically, myelin, the fatty tissue that is wrapped around some nerve cells and is essential for their proper functioning. The strategy is to identify those T cells and make monoclonal antibodies that inactivate them. In 1988, immunologists at Stanford University reported successful use of that strategy in mice that had been given a disease resembling multiple sclerosis.

In an earlier experiment, the same researchers produced antibodies that knocked out too many T cells and killed the mice.

They succeeded only after they found the antigen that identified the clone of T cells that attacked myelin in these mice. Once they found it, they could make the right antibody and stop the damage—without disrupting the immune defenses. When they reported their breakthrough, the scientists carefully noted that they had not identified the multiple sclerosis antigen in human patients, but their work obviously points in that direction.

In theory, monoclonal antibodies could be used to treat almost any autoimmune disease. If an autoimmune disease results from a mistaken attack by T cells against one of the body's tissues, as indeed appears to be the case, the damage could be prevented if physicians identify the receptor on the T cells responsible for the attack and inactivate the faulty T cells with monoclonal antibodies that work against that particular receptor. As of 1989, researchers were trying to develop monoclonal antibody treatments for rheumatoid arthritis, a disease that destroys the tissues of knuckles, knees, and other joints.

There is speculation that a new strategy, though still based on monoclonal antibody technology, can be used to fight the human immunodeficiency virus (HIV) that causes AIDS. This virus does its damage by killing T cells, to which it attaches itself with the help of a receptor on the T cell called T4. If the T4 receptor could be blocked by some harmless molecule, the T cell would be safe from attack by the HIV.

One possible way to protect T cells from the HIV would use what are called anti-idiotype antibodies. (*Idiotype* is another name for *epitope*.) An anti-idiotype antibody is made in a two-step process. The first step is to make a monoclonal antibody. The second is to make an antibody to that antibody. The shape of the second antibody will be identical to the shape of the original antigen. In the case of the HIV, the theory is that this second antibody, which has exactly the same shape as the T4 receptor of the T cells, will bind to the HIV, preventing it from infecting cells.

The same principle lies behind another proposed line of attack. It uses a protein called CD4, which is a synthetic version of the T4 receptor. According to the proponents of this approach, the HIV will attach itself to CD4 and thereby will be rendered harmless.

There is also hope that monoclonal antibodies can help fight cancer. When a normal cell becomes cancerous, its antigens change. Put simply, the theory holds that monoclonal antibodies should allow destruction of the cancer cells, yet leave normal cells unharmed. As of 1989, a great deal of research effort was spent deploying monoclonal antibodies in the war on cancer.

The field of cancer immunology is one of the most active in biomedicine, so active that it requires an entire chapter. But first, the other molecular weapons housed in the immune system must be explored.

·   ·   ·   ·

CHAPTER 4

· · · · · · · · · · · · · · ·

MORE
MOLECULES

Researchers examine activated macrophages.

Antibodies are the most prominent of the immune system's molecules, but many other molecular components are also essential to the system. A great number of them have only recently been discovered. Others have been known for decades. The best place to start is with molecules that were discovered first. The discussion will then move on to the newly recognized ones.

When an antibody combines with an antigen it can immediately trigger action by the complement system, which is a set of at least 20 interrelated immune system proteins. The complement system has been studied in exhaustive detail. Each of its components has been numbered and labeled, and its operations can be described step-by-step.

THE COMPLEMENT SYSTEM

The system can be activated in two ways. Biologists call these routes to activation the classical pathway and the alternative pathway. The classical pathway (so named simply because it was discovered first) is taken when an antigen and an antibody combine to form an antibody-antigen complex. The alternative pathway is triggered by the presence of certain substances, for instance, the toxins produced by some bacteria. Both pathways consist of a cascade of molecular actions, in which one complement protein acts on another, which acts on another, and so on. The two pathways eventually merge. Each, however, has its own set of proteins.

Complement Proteins

Complement proteins do lots of different things, sometimes alone, sometimes in concert with immunoglobulins. When someone suffers a violent allergic reaction, it is because one complement protein of the classical pathway has swung into action, making smooth muscle contract and blood vessels become leaky so that large amounts of histamine are released. This is called an anaphylactoid reaction. If kept under control, it can be a useful defense mechanism in certain situations. If it gets out of control, as in an allergic reaction against penicillin or some other allergen, it can be fatal.

A standard example of a classical pathway reaction is the destruction of incompatible red blood cells. Blood typing has become so commonplace that most people know their blood type— A, B, AB, or O. These types are based on the presence or absence of certain antigens in the membrane of red blood cells. The reaction against blood cell antigens is caused by two complement proteins of the classical pathway acting together with IgG.

Other complement proteins stimulate phagocytes and other white blood cells, break open bacterial cells, help neutralize viruses, attack foreign tissue, and do other essential functions.

Cytokines

Researchers have known about the complement system since the beginning of the 20th century. A new set of immune system molecules was first discovered in the 1950s, and it did not come more fully to light until the 1980s. Indeed, knowledge of the molecules is so new that the nomenclature is still in the process of settling down. The most general name for them is *cytokine*, which denotes a chemical messenger produced by an immune cell, though if it is produced by a lymphocyte, it is called a lymphokine. Cytokines include monokines, interferons and interleukins. When they show up in cancer therapy, they are referred to as biological response modifiers. Scientists and doctors are excited by cytokines because they are essential to the immune response and because their practical uses, now that biologists that manufacture them at will and manipulate them, seem limitless.

One lymphokine that gave researchers a surprise is called tumor necrosis factor, which was first identified as a protein that could kill cancer cells. In the early 1980s, large amounts became available through genetic engineering, and testing it as a cancer treatment began. A strange coincidence was discovered when studies of tumor necrosis factor by other researchers revealed cachexia, a condition that can occur in cancer. Cachexia makes body tissue almost melt away; it is the reason why some cancer patients are so gaunt and starved looking. In the 1980s, researchers found the protein cachexin, which causes cachexia. They were amazed to learn that tumor necrosis factor and cachexin are identical. As of 1989, they were still trying to work out the whys and hows of this powerful, two-edged sword.

All these cytokines are proteins that immune system cells produce to send signals to other immune system cells. Lymphokines from helper T cells tell B cells to make antibodies; activate killer T cells; and stimulate macrophages into action. Some cytokines stimulate the production of white or red blood cells, some attack cancer cells directly, some kill viruses.

The cytokine story began with the discovery by two British scientists in 1957 of a molecule produced by cells in response to infection by a virus. The scientists, Alick Isaacs and John Lindenmann, found that the substance did not kill viruses directly but instead prevented them from reproducing inside infected cells. They called the molecule interferon.

Interferons

For years, interferon remained a curiosity. The only way to obtain it was to extract it from human cells, and the yield was excruciatingly small. Scientists knew it was potentially important, but they could not study it enough because it was very scarce and expensive. Two developments broke the logjam.

One was the discovery in 1977 by Hans Stander in Stockholm, Thomas Merigan of Stanford University, and other researchers, that interferon could slow the growth of cancer in animals, a breakthrough that led cancer patients to demand interferon at any price. Thus, millions of dollars were thrown into interferon research. For two or three years, those millions were spent on the painfully slow extraction of interferon from human cells grown in the laboratory.

Then, in the early 1980s, two biologists, Paul Berg of Stanford University and Herbert Boyer of the University of California at San Francisco, developed genetic engineering, which makes possible large-scale production of interferon and many other proteins. A researcher isolates the gene for the protein, clones it, puts it into bacteria, and grows large amounts of the bacteria. Genetic engineering is not as inexpensive as scientists had originally hoped, but it has solved the interferon shortage—or, rather, interferons: It turns out that the molecule discovered by Isaacs and Lindenmann belongs to a large family. Humans have three kinds of interferons, alpha, beta, and gamma, which bind to different cell receptors. There are at least 15 alpha interferons and one each of beta and gamma. They are being tested against cancer and other diseases, though so far, the results have been disappointing.

One unfulfilled hope was that an interferon, being a natural substance, would cause no negative side effects. Unfortunately, it leads to chills, fever, and aches, perhaps because interferons are naturally made in very small amounts and the body reacts adversely to the large amount used for treatment. Nevertheless, the molecule is being tested as a treatment for several diseases, ranging from leprosy to the common cold. The first trials of an interferon nasal spray, which were done by Thomas Merigan, seemed promising until researchers saw that after four or five days, the treatment caused side effects that were worse than the original cold symptoms.

Slow as the progress has been, interferons still greatly interest cancer researchers. In 1988, an alpha interferon was approved for treatment of a rare kind of cancer, hairy-cell leukemia, named for the kind of white blood cell that proliferates abnormally in this disease. It affects about 2,000 Americans each year.

FDA commissioner Dr. Frank Young speaks at a press conference on the use of interferons to treat hairy-cell leukemia, a rare kind of cancer. Use of genetically engineered interferons was approved in 1988.

Interleukins

The first interleukin was discovered in 1972 by Byron Waksman and Igal Gery in 1972, researchers at Yale University. They grew macrophages in a broth, removed them, and then added T cells. They expected the T cells to die but found instead that a substance that had been secreted by the macrophages caused the T cells to multiply. Waksman and Gery called the substance a lymphocyte-activating factor; now it is called interleukin-1, IL-1 for short. Other interleukins have since been discovered. As of 1989, the series went up to IL-6.

Interleukin-1 induces fever, fatigue, and sleep (helpful effects during an illness); activates bone cells; induces the breakdown of muscle cells; and stimulates T cells to multiply and produce various substances, including interferons and IL-2—now considered the most important of the interleukins.

Dr. Robert Gallo and his fellow researchers at the National Cancer Institute identified the first proven human-cancer virus. Gallo was also one of the first scientists to identify HIV as the cause of AIDS.

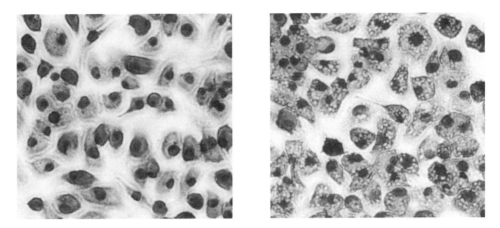

The photo on the left shows macrophages grown with CSF-1, a colony stimulating factor that controls the development of macrophages. The photo on the right shows CSF-grown macrophages ingesting yeast.

Interleukin-2 acts on stimulated T cells that are bound to antigens, increasing their multiplication and their production of interleukin, including more IL-2. One of its properties is to activate killer T cells so they destroy cancer cells, something that makes it one of the most exciting subjects of cancer research, as will be shown in Chapter 7. The ability of IL-2 to make T cells multiply has already helped produce two major advances. One was the identification of the first proven human cancer virus by Robert Gallo and his colleagues at the National Cancer Institute. Called HTTLV-1, the virus causes a T-cell leukemia. The other advance was made by Gallo and by a team led by Luc Montagnier at the Pasteur Institute in Paris, all of whom identified HIV as the cause of AIDS. That achievement would not have been possible without the use of IL-2 to stimulate multiplication of the helper T cells that HIV attacks.

Interleukin-3 is made by lymphocytes and stimulates multiplication of stem cells in the bone marrow. As of 1989, the functions of all the other interleukins were still being explored.

Colony Stimulating Factors

Another newly discovered family of lymphokines consists of colony stimulating factors (CSFs), so named because they were discovered through their ability to make cell colonies grow in the laboratory. One CSF that is already being used medically is erythropoietin, which stimulates production of red blood cells. It has been administered to, among others, artificial kidney patients, who often suffer chronic anemia.

Erythropoietin is not part of the immune system, but some CSFs are. They stimulate production of white blood cells in the bone marrow, thus bolstering immune defenses in times of need. Interleukin-3 can be described as a CSF because it promotes the growth of phagocytes and red blood cell precursors. Other CSFs include CSF-1, which controls the growth and development of macrophages and other monocytes; granulocyte CSF, which stimulates multiplication of granulocytes; and GM-CSF, which stimulates both granulocytes and macrophages. It seems certain that other CSFs will be discovered and put to use.

Colony stimulating factors interest physicians because they can help patients whose immune response is weakened by disease, surgery, transplantation, or drug treatment. Cancer researchers are putting them to two uses. One is to fight leukemias and lymphomas, which are cancers of the white blood cells. Monoclonal antibodies that work against CSFs have been used to stop proliferation of cancerous white cells. In drug treatment of other cancers, the positive side of CSFs is proving valuable. In cases in which doctors must limit doses of anticancer drugs, which can destroy white blood cells and leave the patient vulnerable to infection, CSFs can restore white blood cell counts to normal, enabling patients to get more intensive drug therapy.

Researchers are just beginning to learn about the properties of lymphokines, but it is already clear that these substances are very powerful. As research into lymphokines continues, more benefits will emerge.

•   •   •   •

. . . .

CHAPTER 5

VACCINES

Dr. Albert Sabin administers an oral polio vaccine.

The history of science is often written in such a way that it seems scientists first find out how some basic mechanism of nature works and then put it to practical use. In fact, the process is often reversed. First, someone makes a practical advance and then scientists find out why it works. Such was the case, for example, with the first and most successful vaccine of all, the smallpox vaccine. It was developed before anyone even knew the immune system existed.

THE FIRST VACCINE

In early times, smallpox was a scourge to humankind, feared not only because it killed so many people but also because its survivors were often disfigured for life. So destructive was smallpox that, in the 17th century, some desperate people infected themselves with material from patients with a light case of smallpox, hoping this tactic would spare them the worst ravages of the disease. Often, the tactic failed.

Then, in the late 18th century, an alert British doctor, Edward Jenner, noticed that country folk often deliberately contracted cowpox in order to ward off smallpox. Jenner began to believe

British physician Dr. Edward Jenner invented and administered the first vaccine—for smallpox—in 1796.

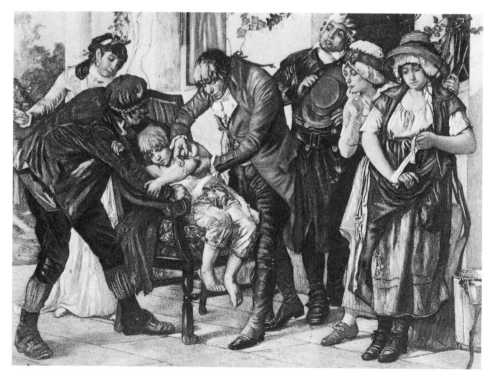

this practice might actually work. In 1796, he performed an experiment that would be unthinkable today. He inoculated an eight-year-old boy—first with cowpox, then with smallpox. The boy did not develop smallpox, and Jenner decided he had hit upon something. He called the procedure vaccination, after vacca, Latin for "cow."

Some doctors resisted the concept of vaccination, but it worked so well that it eventually was adopted everywhere. And two centuries later, Jenner's innovation accomplished what once would have seemed a miracle: In 1977, a concerted vaccination campaign launched by the World Health Organization (WHO) succeeded in wiping smallpox from the face of the earth.

Stalled Progress

For more than a century, Jenner's success led to no further breakthroughs. The smallpox vaccine worked, but no one knew why. Luck, rather than scientific method, had enabled Jenner to stumble onto a virus, cowpox virus, that resembled the smallpox virus enough to stimulate an immune response and yet cause no harmful symptoms. Not until scientists understood the principles behind vaccination could they develop today's vaccines.

An Accident of Genius

The next major advance in vaccines also resulted from an accident—the sort of accident, however, that usually seems to befall only a genius. The genius was Louis Pasteur, a French chemist born in 1822. One of his most revolutionary achievements was something now taken for granted: The idea that many diseases are caused by tiny organisms, which Pasteur called germs, a word no longer used by scientists but still a fixture of everyday speech. Pasteur's concept of germs enabled him and other researchers to plan ways of killing, inactivating, or containing disease. And this seemingly simple idea remains a cornerstone of modern medical theory.

Pasteur's fortuitous accident occurred when he was working on chicken cholera, a deadly disease caused by a bacterium. He was injecting chickens with a virulent strain of the bacterium

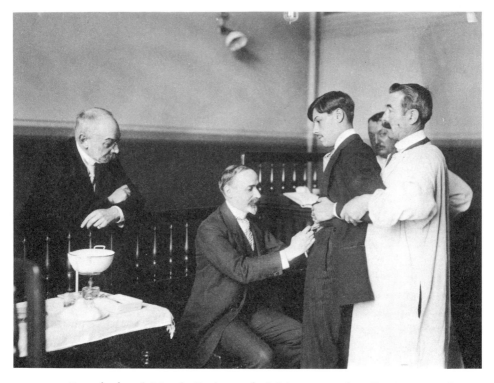

French chemist Louis Pasteur administers a vaccine. Pasteur was the first to develop an attenuated vaccine, which uses weakened strains of bacteria or viruses.

that routinely killed these creatures. One day, however, he mistakenly used some strains that had been standing in the laboratory for a week. To his surprise, the chickens he injected survived exposure to the virulent strain. He realized the bacteria had weakened: They had lost the power to make the chickens sick but retained the ability to arouse the fowls' B cells and T cells, priming them to attack once the deadly strain appeared. Pasteur had lucked into a principle that ruled vaccine development for the next century.

A patient's immune system can also be aroused if he or she is injected with killed, rather than weakened, microbes. Today, one of the two varieties—killed or weakened—is used in all vaccines.

In the case of polio, both types work. The Salk vaccine uses killed poliovirus; the Sabin vaccine uses weakened, or attenuated, strains.

The first attenuated vaccine was developed by Pasteur against rabies, then called hydrophobia. The ailment offered a strong challenge to the chemist because it is caused by a virus, which is much smaller than a bacterium. Using a microscope, Pasteur could see the bacteria that caused chicken cholera. But he could not glimpse the rabies virus. A bacterium is a living organism, a single cell that eats and reproduces in its own primitive way. A virus consists only of a core of genetic material wrapped in a protein coat. It can reproduce only by invading a cell and taking over the cell's metabolic machinery. Bacteria can be grown in the laboratory by giving them the simple food they need. Viruses can be grown only in living cells.

Pasteur did not know he was dealing with a virus, but he knew he was working with an infectious agent. He grew the virus by injecting material from an infected animal into another animal and then continued the process hundreds of times. Eventually, he had material that not only left the animal healthy but also protected it against an injection of the original, virulent material. In 1885, Pasteur used the technique for the first time on a human patient, an eight-year-old boy who had been bitten by a rabid dog. Rabies is almost always fatal, but death does not occur for several weeks after infection. Pasteur's injections saved the boy's life, and the rabies vaccine used today is essentially the one he developed.

VACCINE PROGRESS

The next advance in immunization helped physicians cure diseases, such as tetanus and diphtheria, that are caused by toxins—poisonous substances secreted by infectious microbes. The man responsible for the advance was Emil von Behring, a doctor in the German army. In 1890, he conceived the idea of neutralizing the toxins with blood serum extracted from infected animals. The first antitoxin von Behring developed was against tetanus. Teaming up with Paul Ehrlich, a renowned bacteriologist, Behring produced an antitoxin against diphtheria, one of the most dreaded childhood diseases of the time. The two researchers did not know that their antitoxin was a collection of immunoglobulins, antibodies that work against the toxin.

Behring and Ehrlich had succeeded in providing what is now called passive immunity, that is, protection for a patient provided by immunoglobulins taken from another person (or animal; the tetanus antitoxin came from horses). Physicians continue to apply the principle of passive immunization, for example, when an injection of gamma globulin is given to someone who has not had the hepatitis vaccine but is exposed to that disease.

Passive immunity fades quickly because the person's system uses up the injected antibodies. In 1923, a French bacteriologist, Gaston-Léon Ramon, showed that the tetanus and diphtheria antitoxins could be inactivated by an injection of formaldehyde or by exposure to heat. Injections of the inactivated toxins stimulate production of antibodies by the immune system, protecting against infection. Today's tetanus and diphtheria vaccines consist of inactivated toxins, called toxoids.

Combating Bacteria and Viruses

Nineteenth-century researchers developed other vaccines against bacterial diseases, notably a vaccine that used killed typhoid bacilli. It was introduced in 1897 by a British bacteriologist, Almroth Writh. Immunization against viral diseases progressed slowly, however. Not until the 1930s did scientists learn much about the nature of viruses or about how to grow them in the laboratory.

Viruses, as has been noted, grow only in cells. This means scientists need to keep tissue alive in the laboratory. In the early 20th century, Alexis Carrel, a Frenchman working in the United States, devised methods for doing this, and in 1931, Ernest Goodpasture at Vanderbilt University in Nashville, Tennessee, showed that viruses could be grown in chick embryos. In 1937, Max Theiler, a bacteriologist working at Rockefeller University in New York City, used these new biomedical advances to produce a vaccine for yellow fever. It consisted of a strain of viruses weakened by many passages through animals and chick embryos.

A New Weapon: Antibiotics

The golden age of vaccine development came after World War II, and the key to success was provided by John Enders and his colleagues at Harvard, who used antibiotics, a new discovery at the time, to grow cells in laboratory cultures and keep them free of bacterial contamination. That achievement made it possible for viruses to be grown in large quantities and led directly to the first vaccine against poliomyelitis, an infectious disease that crippled 50,000 Americans in an epidemic year such as 1955.

The first polio vaccine was the brainchild of Jonas Salk, an immunologist at the University of Pittsburgh who in 1954 inactivated the poliovirus with formaldehyde. Soon another researcher, Albert Sabin, developed an attenuated polio vaccine.

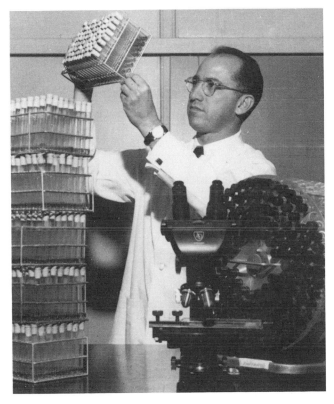

In 1954 Dr. Jonas Salk, an immunologist at the University of Pittsburgh, invented the first polio vaccine. Salk's solution used a strain of the virus that had been inactivated with formaldehyde.

In two or three years, polio was no longer a major medical problem.

Sabin's vaccine is the one most children get today. It can be taken by mouth, whereas the Salk vaccine must be injected. And because the attenuated virus is still alive, it can spread to people who have not been immunized, protecting them as well. No immunization program can reach everybody, but if enough people are immunized even the unprotected benefit from what is called herd immunity: An epidemic cannot happen because so few people are vulnerable to the virus. A live virus vaccine makes it easier to achieve herd immunity.

Vaccines against other common viral childhood diseases—measles, mumps, and rubella (German measles)—came along in the 1960s and 1970s. They joined a vaccine against pertussis, or whooping cough. Children today usually get the diphtheria, pertussis, and tetanus vaccines together in a DPT shot. The recommended immunization schedule for children is for a DPT shot and oral polio vaccine at ages two months and four months, with a third DPT shot at six months. A combined measles-mumps-rubella vaccine is given at ages 12 to 15 months. Polio and DPT boosters are given at 18 months and again when the child enters school, at ages 4 to 6. The tetanus vaccine is given after 10 years of age, and tetanus and diphtheria boosters should be given every 10 years for life.

Late-breaking Vaccines

Several new vaccines have been developed recently. One combats a bacteria, *Haemophilus influenzae*, which can cause meningitis. A second is for hepatitis B, a serious liver disease. The first hepatitis vaccine ever developed used antigens extracted from the blood of people infected with the disease. A newer one holds the distinction of being the first to be produced by genetic engineering. It was made by the American bacteriologist B. S. Blumberg, who cloned the gene for a hepatitis antigen, inserted it in bacteria, and then grew the bacteria. Because the hepatitis vaccine is very expensive, it is given only to people, such as health-care workers, who are at high risk of infection. As of 1989, researchers were developing a vaccine against chicken pox.

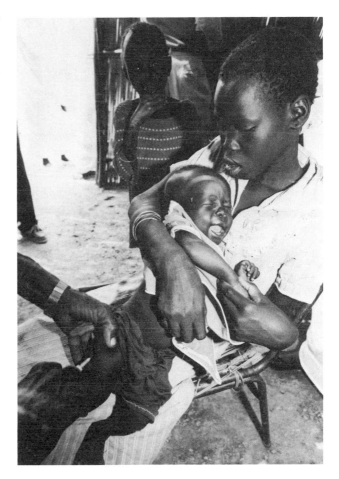

A Sudanese child squirms in his mother's lap while receiving a measles vaccine. Physicians recommend that all children between the ages of 12 and 15 months receive a combined measles-mumps-rubella vaccine.

THE PUZZLE OF AIDS

The greatest challenge for vaccine research now is AIDS. Researchers are reluctant to use the whole virus, either killed or attenuated, for fear that either might cause the disease. Most work is concentrated on finding an epitope (fragment) of a viral coat protein that will induce an immune response. Preliminary human tests of such a vaccine began in 1988, and a number of other such vaccines are under development.

A second approach that could be applied to a number of diseases in addition to AIDS uses Jenner's original discovery, the cowpox virus. The virus is so large that several genes can be put into it. If those genes produce antibodies to HIV and other viruses, it would be possible to immunize people against several diseases with one vaccination. Human tests of an AIDS vaccine using a genetically engineered cowpox virus began in 1988. The year before, in one of the boldest experiments in medical history, Daniel Zagury, a French researcher, inoculated himself and several colleagues with the same sort of vaccine. Tests showed that the volunteers had antibodies to HIV, but as of 1989 it was not certain that the immune response is enough to protect against infection.

AIDS presents other challenges to researchers trying to develop a vaccine. A major problem is that the virus has many strains, and most are mutating rapidly. A vaccine that works against one strain might not protect against others—and the first strain might mutate enough to elude the vaccine. Another issue is that no animal gets AIDS (although the most expensive and valuable research animal of all, the chimpanzee, can be infected with the virus), which makes it difficult to test new approaches in realistic situations. But AIDS vaccine researchers are pushing ahead as rapidly as they can, hoping the biomedical technology of this century can give them an innovative solution.

•　　　•　　　•　　　•

CHAPTER 6

IMMUNE DISEASES

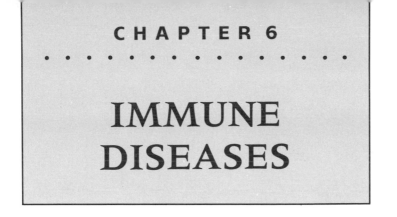

Scientists conduct hypersensitivity disease research.

When the end of summer approaches, about one American in five begins weeping and sneezing. This time of the year is known as hay fever season, although hay has nothing to do with it; the symptoms are the result of pollen from ragweed plants, which cause the most common allergy in the United States. Because so many people suffer from hay fever and other allergies, the periodic discomfort is often endured as a matter of course. But allergies are actually something unusual, an example of a class of medical conditions that affect almost everyone sooner or later—problems caused by the malfunctioning of the immune system.

HOW ALLERGY HAPPENS

Allergy is caused when the immune system mistakenly attacks a harmless invader. The discussion of antibodies in Chapter 3 noted that immunoglobulin E (IgE) specializes in attacking invading parasites. That useful defense mechanism becomes a problem, however, when it singles out an antigen such as ragweed pollen, animal hair, mold spores, insect venom, or penicillin. In all these cases, IgE molecules recognize an antigen and form a bridge between it and a mast cell or basophil, triggering the cell to release mediators such as histamine.

Histamine and Its Effects

Histamine creates several effects, none particularly pleasant. It makes some blood vessels leak fluid, leading to swelling, itching, and inflammation. It causes contraction of smooth muscle, the

A young boy receives an allergy shot. An allergy occurs when the immune system mistakenly attacks a harmless invader, for reasons scientists do not yet know.

kind that lines the airways, and results in wheezing. It increases secretion of thin, watery mucus, making noses and eyes drip. These actions can be beneficial because they can help the body repel a dangerous invader. But when they are not needed, these symptoms can be annoying or worse.

Other Mediators

Histamine is the best-known mediator but it is not the only one. People with allergies know that antihistamines usually give only partial relief. New hope may come from many of the mediators identified in recent years. They belong to a family called leukotrienes, and it is believed that leukotriene-neutralizing drugs might prove valuable as antihistamines. For this reason, many laboratories are trying to develop useful antileukotrienes.

The Perils of Anaphylaxis

Allergic reactions usually occur in the nose and throat, eyes, skin, and other localized areas. The most dangerous reaction is a condition called anaphylaxis, or anaphylactic shock, an explosive release of mediators that occurs in the entire body. Anaphylaxis can be caused by a reaction to insect venom, penicillin or other drugs, some foods, and other allergens. At its worst, anaphylactic shock can kill. The risk of death from anaphylaxis is estimated at 1 in 2.5 cases per year.

THE CAUSES OF ALLERGY

Researchers do not fully understand the causes of allergy. A genetic factor is clearly present because allergies tend to run in families. Inheritance does not tell the whole story, however. A child with an allergic parent will not necessarily develop an allergy. It is more accurate to say that some people inherit a tendency toward allergy, though no one can predict if an allergy will develop or exactly what a person will be allergic to. Environmental factors also seem significant for the obvious reason that allergy-prone people react to whatever allergens they encounter.

A Curious Link

The link between allergy and asthma is also something of a puzzle. Asthma is a breathing problem caused by constriction of the bronchi, the airways leading to the lungs. Asthma is often linked to allergy, but many patients with asthma have no allergy, and asthma attacks can be brought on by nonallergic causes such as exercise, cold air, or stress. It is not clear what role the immune system plays in asthma.

Much of the puzzle of allergy and asthma has been solved, however, and some effective preventive measures and treatment for both conditions are available. One mainstay of treatment is antihistamine drugs. And allergy shots, in which small amounts of the problem-causing allergen are injected in the patient over a period of months or years, can prevent attacks. These shots work by inducing production of IgG antibodies against the allergen. The IgG antibodies neutralize the antigen before it can trigger the IgE response.

AUTOIMMUNE DISEASES

Allergy, in which a person's immune system mistakenly reacts against an innocent invader, can be damaging enough. Imagine how much greater the harm is when the immune system goes haywire and reacts against the body's own cells. This happens surprisingly often, and the result is an autoimmune disease.

As researchers have learned more about the immune system, the list of autoimmune diseases has lengthened. The term once covered only conditions such as multiple sclerosis, in which the fatty sheath around nerves is the target, and myasthenia gravis, in which some essential proteins of the muscle system are destroyed. Now the list includes rheumatoid arthritis, which affects at least 1 in every 100 Americans, and type I diabetes, in which the body fails to manufacture insulin, an essential hormone. There may also be an autoimmune factor in type II diabetes, in which the body cannot make proper use of insulin, but it is not a predominant cause of the ailment.

In recent years, scientists have gotten some inklings about the causes of autoimmune diseases. It seems that the defect does not trace to a single cause but, rather, to an interlocking set of genetic, molecular, cellular, and environmental factors.

A hypersensitivity disease researcher works on an arthritis-related test. Rheumatoid arthritis is just one of several autoimmune diseases, which result when the immune system attacks the body's own cells.

The Role of T Cells

Part of the answer lies in the development of T cells. The discussion of T cells in Chapter 2 mentioned that they mature in the thymus, where they learn to recognize the body's cells as friendly. Specifically, T cells learn to recognize the two types of major histocompatibility complex (MHC) antigens: the type 1 MHC antigens that almost all cells carry; and the type 2 antigens carried by immune system cells such as macrophages. T cells are trained to leave the body's type 1 antigens alone and to mobilize for attack when they spot a cell with a foreign type 1 antigen or the combination of a type 2 antigen and a foreign antigen on the surface of a macrophage or similar cell.

Scientists suspect that one cause of autoimmune disease is that in certain people, some T cells do not learn their lesson well enough. They come out of the thymus with a tendency to recognize the body's type 1 antigens as foreign. In most cases, it is believed, it also takes some kind of stimulus, such as infection by a virus, to make such a T cell attack friendly tissue. The genetics of the immune system is also a factor.

Antigen Genes

Just as there are many different MHC antigens (which is why one person rejects another person's tissue), so there are many different MHC antigen genes. A simple test indicates what kind of MHC genes each person carries. If that test is run on someone with an autoimmune disease, interesting relationships show up. People with type I diabetes tend to have one kind of MHC gene, people with ankylosing spondylitis (a type of arthritis) tend to have another kind, and so on. No one has yet explained those relationships, but it is clear that genes play a role in the auto-immune drama.

So do cells, as shown by work reported in 1988 by Marc Feldmann, a research immunologist in England who has studied thyroiditis, an autoimmune disease in which thyroid gland cells are destroyed, and rheumatoid arthritis, in which the target is the synovial membrane, the tissue that lines the joints. In both diseases, Feldmann reported, cells that should carry only type 1 MHC antigens, which warn away T cells, also carry type 2 antigens, which signal an attack if a foreign antigen is also present.

Why Cells Err: A Scenario

Feldmann and his colleagues say the type 2 antigens are not imported from other parts of the body but, rather, are manufactured by the thyroid cells or synovial joint cells. The researchers have yet to establish why these cells make this elementary mistake, but they have uncovered enough information for a plausible scenario.

It goes like this: An innocent cell mistakenly displays a type 2 antigen, which waves a red flag to prowling T cells. The addition of a foreign antigen, provided perhaps by a wandering virus or bacterium, may be all that is needed to send T cells on the attack. A badly trained T cell requires even less provocation. It simply mistakes a friendly antigen for an enemy. It is also possible that a combination of triggering factors sets the T cell off. In any case, the result is a full-fledged immune attack on friendly tissue, in which such cytokines as interferons, interleukin-1, and tumor necrosis factor possibly cause much of the damage.

Preventive Measures

The scenario is convincing but unproven. Nonetheless, some researchers think they have learned enough about autoimmune diseases to test some preventive measures. In 1987, French researchers declared they had prevented (or at least delayed) type I diabetes in some children by giving them a drug called cyclosporine when the first symptoms appeared. Cyclosporine prevents transplant rejection by neutralizing T cells; in these cases, it apparently prevented T cells from attacking insulin-producing cells. Controversy surrounds the treatment because doctors worry about the long-term effects of cyclosporine on children. But at least it provides a ray of hope.

Severe combined immunodeficiency disorder, SCID, can be fatal unless extraordinary measures are taken. Bone marrow transplants, such as the one shown here, can arrest the disorder but are risky in and of themselves.

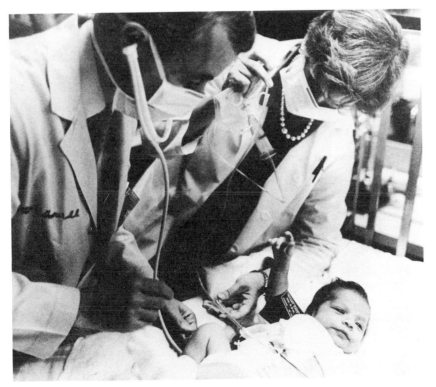

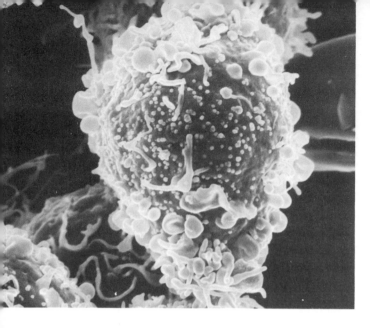

A scanning electron micrograph of what is believed to be an HIV-infected cell. Many scientists fear that almost everyone infected with HIV will develop AIDS.

New Frontiers

There is more to the autoimmune story. One fascinating line of recent research has explored the relationship between the immune system, learning disability (LD), and left-handedness. In 1982, Harvard researcher Norman Geschwind asserted that learning disabilities such as dyslexia (the perceived reversal of letters, which causes reading problems) occur 12 times more commonly among left-handed children than right-handed children. In addition, boys suffer LDs more often than girls, and people with learning disabilities also have a high frequency of immune disorders.

These facts can all be linked in the following way. Human language function is controlled by the left side, or hemisphere, of the brain. Should that hemisphere be damaged, not only would language disabilities (such as dyslexia) ensue but predominance could also be switched to the right hemisphere, which controls the left side of the body. Should an autoimmune reaction related to levels of testosterone, the male sex hormone, be responsible for the damage, boys would be more likely to suffer than girls.

There is evidence to support Geschwind's hypothesis, but as of 1989 it was still being tested on laboratory mice bred to develop autoimmune disease. This theory shows how researchers are looking for immune system involvement in many apparently unrelated disorders, a topic covered at greater length in Chapter 8.

IMMUNE DEFICIENCY DISEASES

Autoimmune disease is caused by an inappropriate immune response. There is another set of disorders caused by a failure of the immune system to respond. These disorders are called immune deficiency diseases.

AIDS

The best-known immune deficiency disease is AIDS. It appears to be one of the deadliest infectious diseases to afflict humankind. Most experts believe that almost everyone infected with HIV will eventually develop AIDS and that almost all of those people will die of it. These assumptions may change as researchers learn more about AIDS and develop treatments for it. After all, its history dates back only to 1981. As yet, however, no other viral or bacterial disease has proved so universally fatal.

AIDS is an unusual immunodeficiency disease because, as its name says, it is acquired—via an infection—and because HIV knocks out the helper T cells. All other such disorders are inherited and result from the inactivation of one part or another of the immune system by natural mechanisms, most not identified as yet.

Other Immunodeficiency Disorders

There are about two dozen immunodeficiency disorders. One such is a condition called agammaglobulinemia, in which the body produces a deficit of immunoglobulins. People afflicted with the ailment suffer repeated infection and other problems. The names of other conditions are self-descriptive: selective IgA deficiency, selective IgM deficiency, and so on. The worst of the lot is severe combined immunodeficiency disorder (SCID), in which the entire immune system essentially does not work. There are several varieties of SCID, but the outcome of all of them is early death unless heroic measures are taken, such as keeping the patient alive in sterile isolation or, in some instances, with a bone marrow transplant.

Bone marrow transplant—in which faulty marrow is destroyed by irradiation and new marrow cells are injected—is risky. The problem is not that the transplanted cells may be rejected but rather that they will reject the rest of the body's tissue, a condition called graft versus host reaction. Thus, a successful marrow transplant requires a very close match between donor and recipient.

Severe combined immunodeficiency disorder is one of the leading candidates for a first attempt at human-gene therapy. The plan is to insert a good gene into faulty bone marrow cells, grow the cells in the laboratory, and then inject them into the patient, where they will multiply and provide a normal immune response. As of 1989, gene therapy was being tested in animals. The techniques remain unperfected, but it is possible that the first human trial could be made in the early 1990s.

It is interesting to note that almost none of this chapter could have been written 30 years ago. If AIDS had come along in the 1950s, it would have been an absolute mystery to biologists. Thanks to basic research on the immune system and clinical work on other immune deficiency disorders, hope glimmers for conquest of this newest, deadly disease.

•   •   •   •

CHAPTER 7

CANCER IMMUNOLOGY

Dr. Steven Rosenberg of the National Cancer Institute.

A lmost every advance in scientists' understanding of the immune system has quickly led to a plan to use the new information in the war against cancer. Alas, the history of cancer immunology has mostly been one of disappointed hopes. Theory after theory has moved to center stage, been tested—and failed. None of the simple strategies has worked. By 1989, new, promising methods had emerged, but it remains to be seen whether they will yield better results than those used in the past.

71

A FERTILE FIELD

The field of cancer immunology was born in the 1950s, when several researchers showed that cancers chemically or virally induced in laboratory animals displayed distinctive antigens. Experiments showed that those tumor antigens caused an immune response, the same kind of attack T cells mount against transplanted tissue, but it lacked the strength to destroy the cancer.

Immune Surveillance

Discovery of tumor antigens led to a theory called immune surveillance. This theory held that from time to time a small number of cells in any person's body could turn cancerous. If the person's immune system was working properly, patrolling immune cells would identify these malignant cells as dangerous invaders and kill them. If the immune response was somehow weakened and could not overpower the first cells that turned malignant, cancer would develop.

This theory also implied a line of attack: If the immune response was pepped up, cancer could be prevented or cured. By the 1970s, several research centers tried that strategy, using many ways of stimulating the immune system. Some investigators injected the bacillus of Calmette and Guérin (BCG), an old (and not very effective) tuberculosis vaccine named for two French doctors. Others tried to make a vaccine formed of antigens taken from a patient's own tumor cells. Still others injected white blood cells from one patient into another.

A parallel effort was led by two Swedish-American researchers, Karl and Ingegerd Hellström. They reported that T-cell attack against cancer cells was blocked by antibodies that bound to the tumor antigens and thus prevented the T cells from reaching the cancer. If the blocking antibodies could themselves be blocked, the Hellströms said, the immune attack could be made effective.

Neither strategy worked, though both achieved limited success. By the end of the 1970s, the effort endorsed by these researchers had been pretty much abandoned along with the theory of immune surveillance. The theory was disproved, first by organ transplants and then by AIDS, which share a common denomi-

Drs. Karl and Ingegerd Hellström believed that cancer cells were normally produced by a healthy body and destroyed; a weak immune system, however, would allow the cancer to develop. This theory, known as immune surveillance, was later proved untrue.

nator, suppression of the immune response—by a virus in the case of AIDS, by drug treatment to prevent rejection in transplantation.

If immune surveillance did indeed exist, transplant recipients and AIDS patients ought to develop a whole range of tumors—cancer of the breast, the colon, the lung, and more. Nothing of the sort has been observed. Transplant patients do have a slightly increased risk of some cancers, largely leukemias and lymphomas. In AIDS patients, the cancer that arises most often is a virulent form of a previously obscure skin tumor, Kaposi's sarcoma, although lymphomas also occur. If there is an immune surveillance system, it is effective only against a small range of cancers.

It is not exactly clear why this is so. One line of research points to the type of antigens produced by cancer cells. Human cancer antigens do not stimulate a strong immune response; T cells do not attack them as they do transplanted tissue. Some studies indicate that cancer antigens are so oddly shaped and incomplete that they escape recognition by the immune system. But, again, the picture is fuzzy.

Hope Dies Again

Tumor antigens aroused another great hope in the 1970s: the hope that cancers could be diagnosed in their early, most curable stage by a simple blood test that could detect specific tumor antigens. Enthusiasm soared when Phil Gold, a researcher at McGill University in Montreal, Canada, announced he had found an antigen that signaled the presence of cancer of the colon. Gold called the antigen carcinoembryonic antigen (CEA) because it resembled an antigen made by fetuses. Gold claimed a positive CEA blood test could indicate the presence of colon cancer before any other symptoms appeared.

That hope, too, was soon dashed. Gold's hypothesis had rested on the belief that CEA was produced only by colon cancer cells. As researchers ran tests, they found that CEA is produced by many other kinds of cells, including lung and pancreas tumors and normal tissues. Carcinoembryonic antigen tests are used today, but they cannot detect early cancers. The amount of CEA is measured during treatment, to see how well a patient responds to therapy—a useful role, but far from the diagnostic break-through first envisioned.

Different Antigens—Same Story

Much the same story can be told about other cancer antigens. At best, they proved to be imperfect tumor markers. One reason is that many tumor antigens are normal products that are man-ufactured in excess by cancer cells. Hence, their appearance alone cannot serve as an early warning sign of cancer. Tests for several of them, however, help doctors gauge the effectiveness of therapy and measure the size of tumors.

The invention of monoclonal antibodies has revived hopes that tumor antigens can be used for early detection. Because mono-clonal antibodies are so specific, researchers have managed to extract from cancer cells a large number of antigens that previously eluded identification. Once again the principle behind this approach is to find an antigen produced by only a specific type of cancer cell. The hope is that monoclonal antibodies can root out even tiny amounts of that antigen in the blood, enabling doctors to detect it at an earlier stage than ever before. A number of laboratories are trying that approach; the jury is still out on their results.

Modest Successes

Monoclonal antibodies have also helped revive the stagnant field of cancer treatment. When monoclonal antibodies first appeared, it was hoped they could be deployed to launch a direct attack against cancer cells. Many researchers produced monoclonal antibodies geared to combat tumor antigens and injected them into

A scientist holds a bottle filled with microcapsules containing monoclonal-antibody-producing cells. Researchers hope that monoclonal antibodies will prove to be a successful cancer-fighting agent.

patients. Some successes were reported, including the cure of a lymphoma patient by Ronald Levy at Stanford University in 1981, but generally the record was one of defeat.

Researchers now agree that monoclonal antibodies alone cannot knock out a cancer, partly because their effect is not powerful enough, partly because they are aimed at what is in effect a moving target. Cancer antigens can change subtly enough to evade attack by a monoclonal antibody, and even if some cells are killed, others appear with different antigens.

Since 1986, scientists have tried new tactics. One is to attach a toxic payload to a monoclonal antibody, which releases it when the antibody reaches a cancer cell. Some researchers attach anticancer drugs, some use radioactive isotopes, and some use ricin, a toxin that penetrates a cancer cell and kills it.

Combined Approaches

Several laboratories are using a combined immunological attack that bolsters the monoclonal antibody with a biological response

Dr. Alan Houghton (left) combined monoclonal antibodies with interleukin-2 to treat melanoma, a deadly cancer. The results of his tests, begun in 1989, are not yet known.

modifier. (A biological response modifier, as mentioned in Chapter 4, is a name cancer therapists have given to cytokines such as interferons or interleukin-2.) In 1989, Stanford researcher Ronald Levy tried using monoclonal antibodies and interferons to combat lymphomas. At the same time, Alan Houghton of New York City's Memorial Sloan-Kettering Cancer Center deployed monoclonal antibodies and interleukin-2 against melanoma, an unusually deadly cancer. Should these or some other combined immunological cancer treatments work, they will make headlines.

Genetic Engineering and Interferons

Some researchers are testing biological response modifiers alone. The first to appear on the scene was an interferon, which in 1978 was heralded as a possible miracle cure for cancer. At the time, it was impossible for that belief to be tested because the interferon had to be extracted painstakingly and expensively from human cells. The advent of genetic engineering made possible large-scale production of interferons, and research soon identified several different kinds of interferons. Since then, alpha, beta, and gamma interferons have been used to treat a large variety of cancers. The results have not measured up to the original high hopes, but they have been good enough to ensure that interferons will play a role in cancer therapy.

At one time, researchers thought large doses of interferons might shrink all tumors, yet spare patients the severe side effects caused by existing anticancer drugs. As it turned out, interferons (and all other biological response modifiers tested so far) have adverse side effects, as was stated in Chapter 4. In addition, interferons are effective against a limited number of cancers. The interferon that has been studied most carefully, alpha interferon, has had no effect on the tumors that have proved the major killers—cancer of the lung, breast, and colon. It has had some effect on lymphomas and kidney cancer and more effect on two fairly uncommon types of leukemia, hairy-cell leukemia and chronic myeologenous leukemia (both named after the affected cells). Alpha interferon achieved a milestone in 1987, however, when it was approved for use against hairy-cell leukemia, which strikes 2,000 Americans each year. It thus became the first bio-logical response modifier to enter ordinary cancer therapy.

A Promising Treatment

Researchers cite several reasons why interferons and other bi-ological response modifiers are less effective then they might be. One reason is that many tumors have poor blood circulation, so only a small amount of an injected interferon reaches them. An-other is that an immune attack against a large tumor is simply not powerful enough to kill all the cancer cells, which may num-ber more than a trillion.

One of the most promising biological response modifier treat-ments employs interleukin-2 and natural killer cells (discussed in Chapter 3). The treatment, developed at the National Cancer Institute by a team headed by Steven Rosenberg, is a complicated one. Because only a small number of killer cells is normally activated by the presence of a cancer, the attack on the tumor is limited. Rosenberg's technique is to remove killer cells from the patient's body, incubate—and activate—them with interleukin-2, then put them back into the patient. The method was first tried in 1985 on 25 patients, all in the first stages of cancer; 3 years later, 8 of them were still alive, and most of the 8 showed no signs of cancer.

The treatment has its drawbacks. It is expensive—it costs about $50,000 per patient—and it can cause severe reactions; the treatment has killed some weaker patients. However, because it has had some success in otherwise untreatable cancers, the National Cancer Institute has set up treatment centers so it can be tested more widely.

Treatment and Risk

Another immunological approach to cancer involves monoclonal antibodies and colony stimulating factors (CSFs), the cytokines that regulate the multiplication of white blood cells. In the late 1980s this approach was being used to make standard cancer drug treatment more effective and less damaging. Cancer drugs kill tumor cells, but they also kill the white blood cells that fight

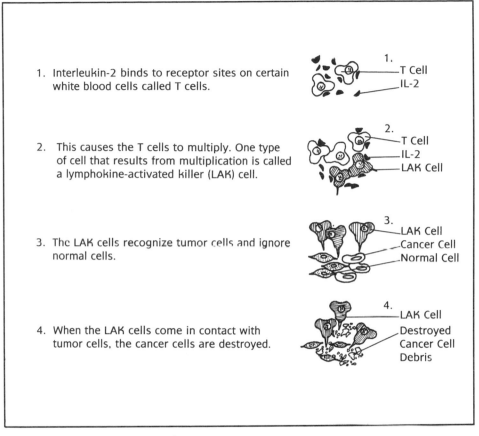

1. Interleukin-2 binds to receptor sites on certain white blood cells called T cells.

2. This causes the T cells to multiply. One type of cell that results from multiplication is called a lymphokine-activated killer (LAK) cell.

3. The LAK cells recognize tumor cells and ignore normal cells.

4. When the LAK cells come in contact with tumor cells, the cancer cells are destroyed.

Interleukin-2 activates the body's immune system to fight cancer.

infection. Many cancer patients undergoing intensive drug treatment now require major transfusions of white blood cells. By increasing white blood cell production, CSFs can reduce the risk of infection and allow doctors to give larger doses of anticancer drugs.

This is the beginning of what promises to be a long story, but for now it appears that, in and of itself, immunotherapy will never be a complete treatment for cancer. Instead, it will probably be incorporated into a combined approach that joins radiation, surgery, and drugs. Perhaps immune treatment will be used to shrink a tumor so that surgery and drug treatment will become more effective. Perhaps after doctors have used other treatments, they will employ immunotherapy to help wipe out the last remaining colonies of cancer cells. In 1989, hundreds of laboratories and hospitals across the globe were ironing out the details.

The immune system has definitely been enlisted in the war against cancer. By the early 1990s, it will be known how much help the immune system can provide.

•　　　•　　　•　　　•

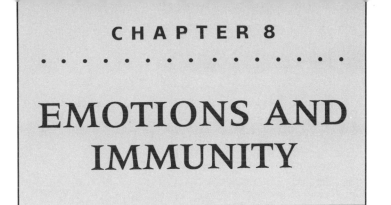

CHAPTER 8

· · · · · · · · · · · · ·

EMOTIONS AND IMMUNITY

There are many stories about someone who died of a "broken heart," passing away a few days after the death of a loved one. Newspapers and magazines run articles about the weakening effects of stress, how health can be affected by one's reaction to events that buffct one's life. And some claim that people can will themselves to health or curb an illness with laughter and a good attitude.

OLD MYTHS AND NEW FACTS

Until recently, many of these stories were dismissed as old wives' tales, but that perception is changing—even among scientists. There is growing evidence that emotions can affect the immune system, weakening or strengthening its defenses. There is even a whole new field—awkwardly titled psychoneuroimmunology— that explores the links between emotions and health.

For a long time, folklore and medical practice have both produced evidence linking the body with the emotions. Folklore abounds with examples of dying people who somehow manage to stay alive until a significant moment—a birthday or an anniversary or the striking of a clock. And it is a known medical fact that a stress can bring on an attack of diseases such as asthma or rheumatoid arthritis. The point is not that patients simply think they have suffered an attack but that their state of mind actually leads to an attack.

New evidence supporting these beliefs stems from research that includes studies of the brain, the nervous system, the hormonal system, and the immune system. Scientists have put several discoveries together and shown how an emotional reaction can trigger brain activity that causes the release of hormones that act on the immune system. Researchers are now trying to determine how this effects sickness and health.

A NEW VIEW OF THE BRAIN

One starting point of the new concept is a picture of the brain that depicts it not only as the seat of thought but also as a gland, an organ that secretes hormones. For many years, the body's master gland was thought to be the pituitary, a small gland that sits at the base of the brain. It is indeed true that the pituitary controls the activity of glands throughout the body. It secretes hormones such as thyrotropin, which stimulates the thyroid; luteinizing hormone, a sex hormone in both men and women; prolactin, which stimulates development of the mammary glands early in a woman's life and milk production after pregnancy; melanocyte-stimulating hormone, which stimulates production of pigment cells in the skin; and—especially interesting to us—

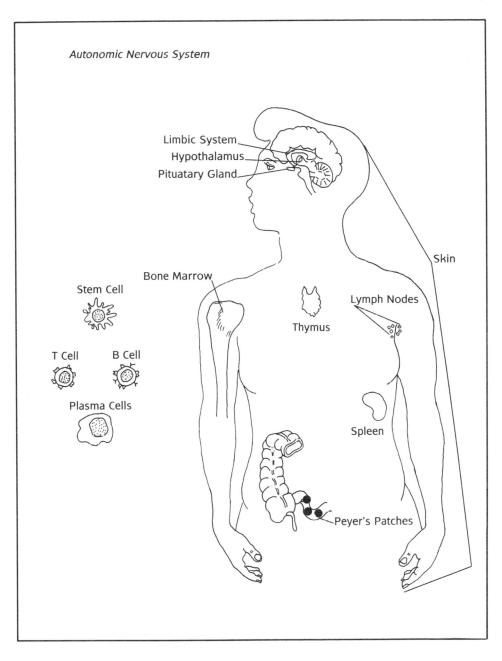

The brain communicates with the immune system through neurotransmitters and immunotransmitters. Scientists feel that a person's emotions can influence his or her health by affecting this intra-body communication.

adrenocortotropic hormone (ACTH), which stimulates hormone secretion by the adrenal glands.

The Hypothalamus

In recent years, however, researchers have found that the master gland is not the pituitary but the hypothalamus, which is a part of the brain. Located at the base of the brain, near the pituitary, the hypothalamus has many connections with the limbic system, the part of the brain that controls emotions. The hormones secreted by the hypothalamus travel to the pituitary, where they regulate the release of pituitary hormones. Eight hypothalamic hormones now have been identified.

Because these hormones are secreted by a part of the brain, their discovery helped connect the first two links of a chain by establishing that brain activity can produce hormonal changes that profoundly affect many physical functions—including the immune response. And that activity springs from a part of the brain, the hypothalamus, which is influenced by emotions, which are themselves controlled by the limbic system.

The Adrenal Glands

As stated, pituitary hormones regulate many functions, including reproduction. What matters here is their effect on the adrenal glands, which sit atop the kidneys and regulate the body's response to emergency situations. The adrenals respond to an emergency by secreting hormones that mobilize the body's defense systems. To say a shock "gets the adrenaline flowing," refers to epinephrine, the technical name for adrenaline, which is one of the hormones released by the adrenal gland. Epinephrine steps up the rate at which the heart beats, increases the amount of blood it pumps, raises blood pressure, and sends a surge of sugar into the blood for energy.

The adrenals also secrete a number of steroid hormones, some of them important in mobilizing for emergency situations. They also directly affect the immune system. Increased secretion of adrenal steroids such as cortisol and cortisone causes the lymphoid tissue of the immune system to shrink. The purpose of this response, it seems, is to release protein that the body might need to repair an injury.

But injury is not the only stimulus for adrenal activity. Any major stress will cause adrenal hormones to surge into the blood. Hence there is a direct physical link between stress—real or imagined—and reduced activity of the immune defense systems.

The Role of Receptors

The final link in this chain is the recent discovery that spleen cells and lymphocytes are equipped with receptors for adrenal steroid hormones, including cortisol, which is secreted as a response to stress. That finding shows that stress can have a direct effect on some of the cells that play major roles in the immune response. In this connection, it is important to remember that each person has his or her own definition of stress. A high school teacher may not think a final exam is stressful, but students usually do. During the exam, the teacher's adrenal function remains stable, whereas the students may produce adrenal hormones at excess speed.

A Second Pathway

Brain activity can influence the immune response through a second pathway. Nerve cells in the brain (and throughout the body) exchange signals by releasing chemicals called neurotransmitters, dozens of which have been identified in different brain pathways. Some of those neurotransmitters, such as epinephrine, are also hormones. Nature thriftily uses the same molecule for different purposes in different parts of the body.

For instance, epinephrine and norepinephrine, its close relative—also secreted by the adrenal glands—act as neurotransmitters in the brain and as stress hormones elsewhere in the body. As such, they participate in a classic feedback loop, in which the concentration of the end product of a production line governs the rate of production, of the sort that is essential if biological responses are to be kept under control. Pituitary hormones stimulate release of adrenal hormones, whose blood levels govern the rate at which the pituitary secretes its hormones. In sum, brain affects body and body affects brain in a loop that profoundly influences immune function.

Important Experiments

These effects have been measured often in animals and humans. In 1988, Bruce Rabin, a researcher at the University of Pittsburgh, reported a typical animal experiment. First he gave laboratory mice a mild electric shock each time they heard a clicking sound. Eventually, the clicking sound alone caused the mice to react fearfully. Rabin then measured specific immune functions, such as lymphocyte activity, in those mice and in a control group. The lymphocytes of the frightened mice did not react and divide as vigorously as those of the normal mice.

In a typical human experiment, researchers at Ohio State University counted natural killer cells in 75 students during their very first semester of medical school and counted them again just before final exams, a particularly stressful time. Cell counts were lower in the examination period, and so were levels of helper and suppressor T cells. In another study, Steven Schliefer of Mount Sinai Medical College in New York City found lower immune system activity in a group of men whose wives had recently died of breast cancer. Immune function did not return to normal level until six months after the wives' death.

Some animal experiments appear to clinch the case by showing that stress can accelerate the process of some diseases. One typical experiment was conducted by Gopi Tejwani, a researcher at Ohio State University who injected rats with a cancer-causing drug. Some rats were stressed by being restrained forcibly for 30 minutes a day. Others were left alone. After 15 weeks, the incidence of breast cancer in the stressed rats had increased by 50%. Tejwani explained the increase by reporting a hormonal link. Stressed rats secreted brain hormones that step up the release of prolactin, the hormone that promotes development of breast tissue during puberty and pregnancy and that is known to stimulate growth of breast cancer.

Outside the Laboratory

The experiments described above have been cited by people who say that cancer is "all in the mind." Some cancer patients have been told they themselves brought the disease on by thinking

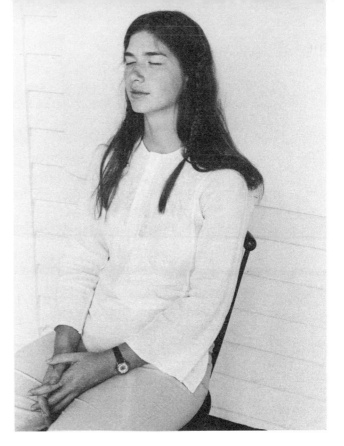

Some people believe that imaging—having a patient picture his or her immune system going into action—can be beneficial. At this time, however, there is little hard evidence to support this theory.

negative thoughts. Others have been told they will get better if they develop appropriate thought patterns.

But it is not that simple. Experimental animals are not humans and laboratory situations are not real life. As of 1989, no relationship had been established between emotional status and cancer cause and cure. Some human studies show a relationship between a cancer patient's state of mind and response to treatment. Most do not. It seems premature to blame cancer patients for negative thinking.

According to Marvin Stein, a research psychiatrist at Mount Sinai Medical Center in New York City, "When a person is under stress, the cerebral cortex [conscious brain] appears to stimulate the hypothalamus, which then activates the hormones and neurotransmitters that act on the immune system." He adds, "But beyond this broad outline of the relationship between the brain and the immune system, the picture becomes fuzzy. It may be that the immune system reacts differently to acute stress and/or chronic stress. And we don't yet know enough about the time course of immune system changes. We need to do repeated studies over longer periods of time with larger groups of patients." Individual reactions also figure in the equation. Some people handle stressful situations better than others, instinctively adopting psychological strategies that help them cope. A study of college students by Harvard University's Steven Looke found the "good copers," those who showed the fewest psychiatric symptoms during stressful life changes, had significantly higher levels of natural killer cell activity than did "poor copers."

Missing Links

But after all the evidence is added together, two final links in the chain are still missing. As of 1989, no researcher had established a direct link between illness and the lowered immune system activity measured in test subjects. What evidence exists is inconclusive. Some studies of bereaved subjects have detected an increase in illness and death; others have not. Most studies that have aimed to relate psychological attitudes to medical outcome in cancer have drawn a blank.

If attitude is ever found to affect sickness and health, the final link in the chain will prove to be a set of strategies that will keep people well and help them fight off illness. For now, it seems such strategies do not exist. Many claims have been made for "imaging"—a patient's effort to picture the body's immune defenses going into action. But hard evidence that it changes the course of cancer and other diseases is woefully scarce. No patient will be harmed by positive thinking, but no scientific proof attests that it helps.

Even so, the mind-body relationship has been proved scientifically, and that fact alone may have great implications. The more scientists know about the immune system and its regulation, the better they will someday be able to stimulate or suppress the immune response in order to fight disease. As of this writing, researchers were seeking to determine whether psychotherapy will be an appropriate immunological treatment in the future. This and other prospects from this chapter form the topic of the book's final chapter.

•   •   •   •

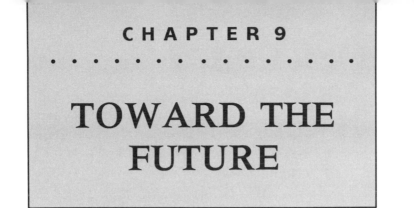

CHAPTER 9

. . . .

TOWARD THE
FUTURE

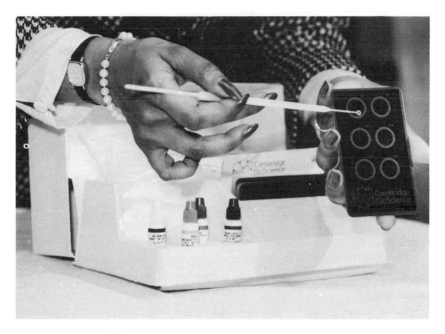

An AIDS testing kit.

The top priority for applied immunology research today is
AIDS. The primary motive is to save lives by finding ways to
prevent and cure the disease. Researchers recognize, however,
that the conquest of AIDS would immensely benefit many other
areas of research and medical practice.

AIDS is a disease in which a central part of the immune system,
the helper T cells, is destroyed by a virus. Study of the disease
has provided major insights into the way helper T cells function

in the immune response. A major goal of AIDS research is to find drugs or other treatments that can increase the activity of helper T cells or prevent their destruction by the virus. If and when that goal is achieved, scientists will have a new way of manipulating the immune response that they could then apply to many diseases, perhaps including some immunodeficiency states.

A WINDOW OF OPPORTUNITY

AIDS provides a grim natural laboratory for studying some fine points of the immune system. For example, the HIV attacks helper T cells because they have a specific receptor, called T4, in their outer membrane. The T4 receptor appears to be essential to the normal activity of helper T cells. The effort now under way to prevent HIV from infecting T cells by blocking the T4 receptor will tell scientists a great deal about this part of the immune system.

Research into possible use of the cowpox virus as the carrier for an AIDS vaccine may well be applied to vaccines in general. As stated in Chapter 5, the cowpox virus is large for a virus—large enough to carry a number of genes inserted into it through genetic engineering. In 1988, genetically engineered cowpox virus vaccines were being tested not only for AIDS but also for influenza, malaria, herpes, and rabies. In theory, at least, it may soon be possible to genetically engineer a cowpox virus that would serve as a vaccine for all these diseases. Creating this all-in-one vaccine is a challenge that will involve researchers for some time to come.

New Discoveries, New Prospects

Another major challenge is to make use of all the cytokines discovered in recent years. Such molecules as interleukin-2 and tumor necrosis factor are being tested on cancer, as noted previously in this book. Another branch of research aims to devise usable drugs from work with leukotrienes, in the same way that valuable pharmaceuticals for allergy, the common cold, and ulcers were developed from work with histamines.

Leukotrienes, like histamines, are mediators released by immune system cells. They are responsible for many of the symptoms of asthma and allergy and also contribute to the inflammation caused by gout, rheumatoid arthritis, and other diseases.

In the early 1980s, when leukotriene research first blossomed, it seemed it would be easy to create useful drugs by developing antileukotrienes. As of 1989 those drugs were still unavailable because the leukotriene story is more complicated than had been thought. There are at least five leukotrienes, and each has a different function within the body. So far, it has not been possible to produce a marketable drug that blocks a specific leukotriene responsible for causing a specific symptom.

Promising Drugs

There are signs of progress, however. Drugs that block a leukotriene, designated D4, have worked well in animals that were experimentally given asthma. Drugs that block leukotriene B4

The vaccinia virus (the basis of the smallpox vaccine) is combined with a hepatitis-B gene. The vaccine produced not only fights smallpox but is effective against hepatitis B as well.

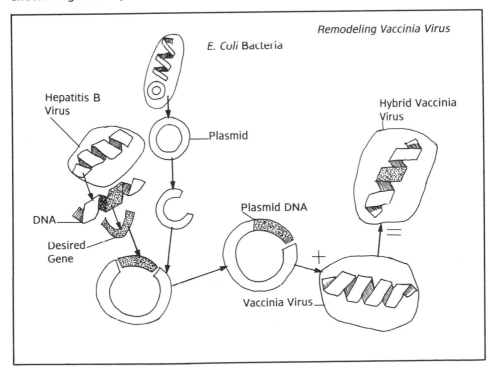

look promising for rheumatoid arthritis and gout, although the work has not advanced beyond its early stages.

The most important fact about immunology research is that it is just beginning. Knowledge about many parts of the immune system—the cytokines and lymphokines, for instance—is only a few years old, and biologists continue to puzzle out the complex relationships between all the cells and molecules that work in concert to defend the body. New phenomena are constantly being discovered. For example, in August 1988, scientists at the University of California at San Diego reported that there appear to be two distinct types of helper T cells. One type, found in lymphoid organs, reacts quickly to infection and secretes interleukin-2 and gamma interferon. The second type, found in the blood, reacts slowly and secretes interleukin-4 and interleukin-5. According to the San Diego researchers, type 1 helper T cells are the cells that remember past infection and respond quickly when the invader appears again—they are thus the key to the success of vaccines—and also spur the inflammatory response at wound sites or organ transplants. The interleukins released by type 2 helper T cells stimulate antibody production by B cells.

Such discoveries show that even after decades of exciting discoveries, immunology research still has a bright future. Some of that research, the applied part, is relatively predictable. Physicians and scientists will continue to try new ways of using all the knowledge they have about the immune system, all the new molecules that are at hand, and all the new methods of biomedical technology to prevent and treat all the diseases in which the immune system plays a role.

Basic research is less predictable. It is impossible to know what new cytokine may be isolated next week or next month, what new interaction between molecule and cell may soon be discovered. The quantity of knowledge gained about the immune system in the past 20 years is impressive. But what fascinates the imagination is all that remains to be learned.

•   •   •   •

APPENDIX:
FOR MORE INFORMATION

The following is a list of organizations and associations that can provide further information on the immune system and the diseases and disorders associated with it. For further information regarding local organizations and treatment centers, please refer to the appendixes in the ENCYCLOPEDIA OF HEALTH volumes *AIDS*, *Organ Transplants*, and *Allergies*.

AIDS Action Council
Federation of AIDS-Related
　Organizations
729 Eighth Street, SE
Suite 200
Washington, DC 20003
(202) 547-3101 or -3102

AIDS Committee of Toronto
66 Wellesley East
Toronto, ONT M4Y 1G2
(416) 926-1626

American Academy of Allergy and
　Immunology
611 East Wells Street
Milwaukee, WI 53202
(412) 272-6071

American Association for Clinical
　Immunology and Allergy
311 Oakridge Court
Bellevue, NE 68005
(402) 292-8950

American Association of
　Immunologists
9650 Rockville Pike
Bethesda, MD 20014
(301) 530-7178

American Board of Allergy and
　Immunology
University City Science Center
3624 Market Street
Philadelphia, PA 19104
(215) 349-9466

American Cancer Society
90 Park Avenue
New York, NY 10016
(212) 599-8200

American Council on
　Transplantation (ACT)
700 North Fairfax Street, Suite 505
Alexandria, VA 22314
(703) 836-4301
(800) ACT-GIVE

American Osteopathic College of
Allergy and Immunology
P.O. Box 8032
West Bloomfield, MI 48304
(313) 280-5800

American Red Cross AIDS
Educational Office
1730 D Street, NW
Washington, DC 20006
(202) 737-8300

American Society for
Histocompatibility and
Immunogenetics
211 East 43rd Street
Suite 301
New York, NY 10017
(212) 867-4193

Arthritis Information Clearinghouse
P.O. Box 9782
Arlington, VA 22209
(703) 558-8250

Centers for Disease Control (CDC)
AIDS Activity
Building 1, Room B-68
1600 Clifton Road
Atlanta, GA 30333
(800) 342-7514

Children's Transplant Association
(CTA)
P.O. Box 2106
Laurinburg, NC 28352
(919) 276-7171

International Association of
Allergology and Clinical
Immunology
611 East Wells Street
Milwaukee, WI 53202
(414) 276-6445

International Society of
Developmental and Comparative
Immunology
Dept. of Anatomy
School of Medicine
University of California
Los Angeles, CA 90024
(213) 825-9567

Joint Council on Allergy and
Immunology
P.O. Box 520
Mt. Prospect, IL 60056
(312) 255-1024

National AIDS Center
Health Protection Building, B-7
Tunney's Pasture
Ottawa, ONT K1A 1B4
(613) 957-1774

National AIDS Network
729 Eighth Street, SE
Suite 300
Washington, DC 20003
(202) 483-7979

National Cancer Institute
National Institutes of Health
9000 Rockville Pike, Building 31,
10A18
Bethesda, MD 20892
(301) 496-5583
(800) 4-CANCER

National Coalition on Immune
System Disorders
P.O. Box 40031
Washington, DC 20816

National Institute of Arthritis and
Musculoskeletal and Skin
Diseases
9000 Rockville Pike
Building 31, Room 9A04
Bethesda, MD 20892
(301) 496-3583

National Multiple Sclerosis Society
205 East 42nd Street
New York, NY 10017
(212) 986-3240

National Organ Transplant
Education Foundation (NOTEF)
1275 K Street, NW
Suite 900
Washington, DC 20005
(203) 371-0393

Ontario Public Education Panel on
  AIDS
15 Ovcrlca Boulevard, 5th Floor
Toronto, ONT M4H 1A9
(416) 965-2168

Pan American Health Organization
525 23rd Street, NW
Washington, DC 20037
(202) 861-4353

United Network for Organ Sharing
  (UNOS)
P.O. Box 28010
Richmond, VA 23228
(800) 24-Donor

U.S. Public Health Service
Office of Public Affairs
Hubert H. Humphrey Building
Room 725-H
200 Independence Avenue, SW
Washington, DC 20201
National AIDS hot line: (800) 342-
  AIDS
(Spanish-speaking operators
  available)

World Health Organization
AIDS Program, Europe

Copenhagen, Denmark
Hot line: 45-1-290-111

World Health Organization
AIDS Program, Geneva,
  Switzerland
Hot line: 41-22-91-21-11

World Health Organization
  Regional Office
P.O. Box 6
Brazzaville, Congo

World Health Organization
  Regional Office
P.O. Box 1517
Alexandria
21511 Egypt

World Health Organization
  Regional Office
World Health House
Indraprestha State
Ring Road
New Delhi, India 110002

World Health Organization
  Regional Office
P.O. Box 2932
Manila, 2801 Philippines

FURTHER READING

Balkwill, Frances. "The Body's Protein Weapons." *New Scientist*, June 1988, 1–4.

Blaiss, Nicholas S., and Clark F. Springate. "Human Immune System Response to Allergens and Anti-Allergenic Agents." *Modern Medicine* 52 (March 1988): 52–55.

Capron, A., et al. "Frontiers in Biology: Immunology." *Science* 238, no. 4830 (November 1987): 1065–98.

Check, William A. *AIDS*. New York: Chelsea House, 1988.

Edelson, Edward. *Allergies*. New York: Chelsea House, 1989.

Facklam, Margery, and Howard Facklam. *Spare Parts for People*. San Diego: Harcourt Brace Jovanovich, 1987.

Gamlin, Linda. "The Human Immune System." Parts 1, 2. *New Scientist*, March 10 and 24, 1988, 1–4, 1–4.

Geha, Raif S. "Regulation of IgE Synthesis in Atopic Disease." *Hospital Practice*, February 15, 1988, 91–102.

Gohlke, Mary, and Max Jennings. *I'll Take Tomorrow*. New York: M. Evans, 1985.

Hancock, Graham, and Enver Carim. *AIDS: The Deadly Epidemic*. London: Victor Gollancz, 1986.

Kantor, Fred S. "Autoimmunities: Diseases of Dysregulation." *Hospital Practice*, July 15, 1988, 75–84.

Kittredge, Mary. *Organ Transplants*. New York: Chelsea House, 1989.

Koop, C. Everett, M.D. *Surgeon General's Report on Acquired Immune Deficiency Syndrome*. Washington, DC: U.S. Department of Health and Human Services, 1987. (This can be obtained free of charge from InterAmerica Research, 1200E North Henry Street, Alexandria, VA 22314, Attention: Clint Jones.)

Leinwand, Gerald. *Transplants: Today's Medical Miracles*. New York: Watts, 1985.

Lockey, Richard F. "Primer on Allergic and Immunologic Diseases." *Journal of the American Medical Association* 258, no. 20 (November 1987): 2894–3034.

Norback, Craig T., and the Asthma and Allergy Foundation of America, eds. *Allergy Encyclopedia*. New York: New American Library, 1982.

Pekkanen, John. *Donor*. Boston: Little, Brown, 1986.

Understanding the Immune System. Bethesda, MD: National Institutes of Health, 1988.

Weir, D. M. *Aids to Immunology*. Edinburgh: Churchill Livingstone, 1986.

GLOSSARY

AIDS acquired immune deficiency syndrome; an acquired defect in the immune system, thought to be caused by a virus (HIV) and spread by blood or sexual contact; leaves people vulnerable to certain, often fatal, infections and cancers

allergy an inappropriate and harmful response of the immune system to normally harmless substances

antibiotic a substance produced by or derived from a microorganism and able in solution to inhibit or kill another microorganism; used to combat infection caused by microorganisms

antibody one of several types of substances produced by the body to combat bacteria, viruses, or other foreign substances

antigen a bacteria, virus, or other foreign substance that causes the body to form an antibody

autoimmune disease a condition in which the immune system attacks the body's own tissues and cells, mistaking them for foreign substances

B cells B lymphocytes; immune system cells that produce IgE

cancer any malignant tumor that, as it spreads to adjacent tissue layers or to other parts of the body, destroys normal tissue

DNA deoxyribonucleic acid; a nucleic acid that is found in genes and is a carrier of genetic information

epitope a unique shape or marker carried on an antigen surface; it triggers a corresponding antibody response; also called idiotype

genes complex units of chemical material contained within the chromosomes of cells; variations in the patterns formed by the components of genes are responsible for inherited traits

histamine the most common mediator, a compound that causes allergic responses

HIV human immunodeficiency virus; the virus believed to cause AIDS

hybridoma a hybrid cell created by the fusion of a normal antibody-producing lymphocyte with a cancer cell; used to produce a specific antibody

IgE a type of immunoglobulin; produced by cells of the lining of the respiratory and intestinal tract; IgE is responsible for some allergic reactions

immune system the body's mechanism for combating viruses, bacteria, and other outside threats; composed of various types of white blood cells, including phagocytes, which consume bacteria, and lymphocytes, which produce antibodies

immunoglobulins globular proteins produced by the immune system to act as antibodies

interferon one of a group of molecules that prevent viruses from reproducing inside infected cells

interleukins a major group of lymphokines and monokines

lymphocyte a type of white blood cell involved in immunity; includes B lymphocytes and T lymphocytes

lymphokines powerful chemical substances secreted by lymphocytes; these soluble molecules help direct and regulate the immune responses

macrophage a type of white blood cell that destroys invading cells by engulfing them

mast cells a granulocyte found in tissue; the contents of mast cells, along with those of basophils, are responsible for the symptoms of allergy

monoclonal antibody a laboratory-made antibody that is used to slow the rejection of a transplanted organ while leaving the rest of the person's immune system intact; its usefulness generally lasts for only a limited period of time

phagocytes large white blood cells that contribute to the immune defenses by ingesting microbes or other cells and foreign particles

RNA ribonucleic acid; a nucleic acid that is found in the cytoplasm and also in the nucleus of some cells; one function of RNA is to direct the synthesis of proteins

T cells T lymphocytes; cells that signal other lymphocytes to attack invading cells or chemical structures foreign to the body

virus a minute acellular parasite composed of genetic material (either DNA or RNA) and a protein coat; viruses cause such diseases as polio, measles, rabies, and smallpox

INDEX

PICTURE CREDITS

Courtesy of American Cancer Society: p. 73; Courtesy of American Council on Transplantation: p. 21; AP/Wide World Photos: pp. 67, 75, 89; The Bettmann Archive: pp. 16, 52, 54; Courtesy of Cetus Corporation: pp. 43, 49; Illustration by Cetus Corporation, as redrawn by Nisa Rauschenberg: p. 79; Courtesy of John Gilroy Photography/The Upjohn Company: p. 61; Courtesy of Dr. Matthew A. Gonda and Dr. Robert C. Gallow: p. 68; Pam Hasegawa/Taurus Photos: p. 62; Courtesy of Christopher Little/Memorial Sloan-Kettering Cancer Center: p. 76; Phiz Mezey/Taurus Photos: p. 81; Computer graphic modeling and photography by Dr. Arthur J. Olson, Scripps Clinic: p. 33; Reuters/Bettmann Newsphotos: pp. 48, 59, 71; Ray Solomon/Monkmeyer Press: p. 87; Courtesy of Roger Ulrich, Ph.D./The Upjohn Co.: p. 23; Courtesy of The Upjohn Co.: pp. 25, 65; UPI/Bettmann Newsphotos: pp. 13, 14, 36, 39, 47, 51, 57; Nisa Rauschenberg: pp. 19, 28, 29, 31, 35, 41, 83, 91

Edward Edelson, author of *Nutrition & the Brain* and *Drugs & the Brain* in Chelsea House's ENCYCLOPEDIA OF PSYCHOACTIVE DRUGS and *Sports Medicine* and *Allergies* in Chelsea House's ENCYCLOPEDIA OF HEALTH, is science editor of the *New York Daily News* and past president of the National Association of Science Writers. His other books include *The ABCs of Prescription Narcotics* and the textbook *Chemical Principles*. He has won awards for his writing from such groups as the American Heart Association, the American Cancer Society, the American Academy of Pediatrics, and the American Psychological Society.

Dale C. Garell, M.D., is medical director of California Childrens Services, Department of Health Services, County of Los Angeles. He is also clinical professor in the Department of Pediatrics and Family Medicine at the University of Southern California School of Medicine and Visiting associate clinical professor of maternal and child health at the University of Hawaii School of Public Health. From 1963 to 1974, he was medical director of the Division of Adolescent Medicine at Children's Hospital in Los Angeles. Dr. Garell has served as president of the Society for Adolescent Medicine, chairman of the youth committee of the American Academy of Pediatrics, and as a forum member of the White House Conference on Children (1970) and White House Conference on Youth (1971). He has also been a member of the editorial board of the *American Journal of Diseases of Children*.

C. Everett Koop, M.D., Sc.D., is Surgeon General, Deputy Assistant Secretary for Health, and Director of the Office of International Health of the U.S. Public Health Service. A pediatric surgeon with an international reputation, he was previously surgeon-in-chief of Children's Hospital of Philadelphia and professor of pediatric surgery and pediatrics at the University of Pennsylvania. Dr. Koop is the author of more than 175 articles and books on the practice of medicine. He has served as surgery editor of the *Journal of Clinical Pediatrics* and editor-in-chief of the *Journal of Pediatric Surgery*. Dr. Koop has received nine honorary degrees and numerous other awards, including the Denis Brown Gold Medal of the British Association of Paediatric Surgeons, the William E. Ladd Gold Medal of the American Academy of Pediatrics, and the Copernicus Medal of the Surgical Society of Poland. He is a Chevalier of the French Legion of Honor and a member of the Royal College of Surgeons, London.